KID POWER

Amazing Things Done by Ordinary Youngsters

Doris Irish Lacks

TEACH Services, Inc.
PUBLISHING
www.TEACHServices.com • (800) 367-1844

World rights reserved. This book or any portion thereof may not be copied or reproduced in any form or manner whatever, except as provided by law, without the written permission of the publisher, except by a reviewer who may quote brief passages in a review.

The author assumes full responsibility for the accuracy of all facts and quotations as cited in this book. The opinions expressed in this book are the author's personal views and interpretations, and do not necessarily reflect those of the publisher.

This book is provided with the understanding that the publisher is not engaged in giving spiritual, legal, medical, or other professional advice. If authoritative advice is needed, the reader should seek the counsel of a competent professional.

Copyright © 2024 Doris Irish Lacks
Copyright © 2024 TEACH Services, Inc.
ISBN-13: 978-1-4796-1764-7 (Paperback)
ISBN-13: 978-1-4796-1765-4 (ePub)
Library of Congress Control Number: 2024910529

All Scripture quotations, unless otherwise indicated, are taken from the New King James Version®. Copyright © 1990 by Thomas Nelson. Used by permission. All rights reserved.

All Scripture quotations marked KJV are taken from the King James Version®. Public domain.

Scripture quotations marked GNT are from the Good News Translation in Today's English Version—Second Edition Copyright © 1992 by American Bible Society. Used by Permission.

Scripture quotations marked MEV are taken from the Modern English Version. Copyright © 2014 by Military Bible Association. Used by permission. All rights reserved.

Scripture quotations marked CW are taken from The Clear Word. Copyright © 2003 by Jack J. Blanco. Used by Permission. All rights reserved.

Published by

www.TEACHServices.com • (800) 367-1844

DEDICATION

To the many "kids" I've known and enjoyed, who are grown up now—Pathfinders who led me out of the woods when I was lost and who called me "Fearless Leader." To the hundreds of my Sabbath School students in America and Africa. Also to my own and my step-grandchildren and great-grands. To my neighbor kids who are always eager to help. Best blessings and success to all of you!

TABLE OF CONTENTS

Appreciation . . . . *vii*

1. History's Bravest—Martin Luther 9
2. Boy Pastor—Ulrich Zwingli. 13
3. Out of the Mouth of Babes—Peter Toussaint 17
4. The Young Amanuensis—Roger Williams. 21
5. Sickly Body, Healthy Brain—Blaise Pascal 25
6. Good News to Planet Earth—Joseph Wolff 29
7. Finger Reading—Louis Braille .35
8. Smart Aleck—Alexander Graham Bell 39
9. And a Merry Christmas to All!—Albert Sadacca 45
10. Before Your TV—Philo Farnsworth 49
11. Writing from the Word Go!—Farley Mowat. 53
12. Written in Secret, Published to the World—Anne Frank. 57
13. I Love the Flag!—Robert G. Heft 63
14. Let There Be Light—Rebecca Schroeder 67
15. Precious Garbage—Favio Chavez 71
16. Child Slaves—Iqbal Masih 75
17. The Invisible Video Tape—Michael Phelps 81
18. The Water Boy—Ryan Hreljac .87
19. The Electronic Brain—Kelvin Doe 91

20. Firsthand—Easton LaChappelle 95
21. The Little Red Wagon—Zach Bonner 101
22. Victim to Victor—Brandon Boynton. 105
23. No Electricity Needed—Ann Makosinski 109
24. No Girls Allowed—Malala Yousafzai 113
25. Warm Homes in Winter—Cassandra Lin 117
26. Gotta Have Sole—Nicholas Lowinger 121
27. The Superkidpreneur—Maya Penn 125
28. Netting the Goal—Rachel Zietz 129
29. Fit to Be Tied—Moziah Bridges 133
30. Smart Kid, Smart Machine—Neil Deshmukh 137
31. Little Girl Inventor—Gitanjali Rao 141
32. Warm Bath—Xochitl Guadalupe Cruz Lopez. 145
33. The Beast—Juniper Netteburg. 149
34. Little Man—Harvey Sutton. 155

APPRECIATION

My most sincere and fondest thanks to my editor, Dr. Brian Strayer, Professor Emeritus of History at Andrews University (retired but not tired) who has never given up on me, despite my knucklehead mistakes in punctuation through the years.

And to my two daughters and their husbands, Sue and Howard Zelener, and Lynn and Ted Elmendorf, who give themselves to helping this 97-year-old mom to navigate without sinking the ship!

Also, my great admiration and thanks for all the talented and hard workers at TEACH Services. And to our magnificent Creator God and His Son, our Redeemer Christ Jesus, and His Holy Spirit who has guided me through thick and thin so that I've been able to come up wavin' the flag!

1
HISTORY'S BRAVEST

1493—Saxony, Germany

He came home from school with red welts on his arms and legs. Mother came from the kitchen and exclaimed, "Martin! Not again?" She bent down to look at his legs. "What did you do this time?"

"Teacher got mad at me for spilling some water. Mama, I didn't do it on purpose."

"And your brothers and sisters come home, and they've been whipped too! We've tried to teach you to be good and courteous at school. What's going on?"

"The teachers are cross and mean all the time. No matter how hard we try, we just can never please them. We all hate school."

So it was in that humble miner's cabin that day—and every day. Ten-year-old Martin thought school must be hell or purgatory. He woke up many nights to hear his father praying for him.

When he turned fourteen, his parents sent him to a school run by the Brethren of the Common Life, a group of Catholic laymen (not priests) who wished to live apart from the world and closer to God. There he learned that because of his sins, he had to perform the most humble and tedious work, going door-to-door begging or singing for food. His gloom darkened because he was taught that God was a severe, stern judge without mercy.

But he told himself, "I have to keep going. There's so much to learn. I want to be useful in my life—stable and solid. But I don't want to be a show-off either." The Lord was leading him step-by-step for a future he could not have imagined.

When he turned eighteen, his father and he talked together. "Son," he said, "I know how hard you've worked and how well you've done in school. Your mother and I have worked hard too. Things are better for us now. I own a mine and a copper smelter. We've saved money from our business, and now I believe I can send you to the University of Erfurt if you'd like to go. You can prepare for law school."

"Oh, Father, thank you! I'll make you proud!"

But he didn't. While at the university library one day, he came across a Latin Bible. He had heard some Scriptures spoken of in public talks, like the Ten Commandments and the Beatitudes, but thought that was the only Scriptures. Now he looked at the entire Bible. His breathing came faster as did his heartbeat. "This is God's Word! All of it! Look! All of this is about Jesus right here! Oh, if I could only have a book like this!" Suddenly, all his dreams and goals changed. He spent all his spare time with that Book, even missing meals and sleep. He loved to compare text with text, and soon everything else lost its importance.

He graduated with a bachelor's degree when he was nineteen. He went on for a master's degree, but the Bible was his first and foremost book which, unknown to him, prepared him for years of conflict with not only his own father but also with the church officials. Even though he eventually became a monk and a professor, he was convinced from his Bible study that his church, the pope, and priests were teaching errors and living immoral lives while leading the people into a godless, hopeless future.

As he taught and preached to the people, they came in droves. They had never heard such deep and practical words that gave them hope in God and in the chance of soul freedom through Jesus. The church leaders saw their funds dwindling as a result (they had been teaching that forgiveness of sin could be bought with money), and they made Martin appear before councils and leaders, but he replied always, "Prove to me from the Scriptures that I am wrong," which they could not do. Soon they conspired to kill him, but he escaped with the help of Frederick III who hid him in Wartburg Castle for a year. During that time, Martin translated the Bible from Latin to German for the people, thus furthering the great Reformation and changing the world.

Martin Luther contributed to the Protestant faith—not by works, but by faith in the Son of God, Jesus Christ, who sacrificed His life for the human race. Luther will be remembered as His servant and friend to the very end.

Martin Luther
1483–1546

"For sin shall not have dominion over you, for you are not under the law, but under grace. What then? Shall we sin because we are not under the law but under grace? Certainly not! Do you not know that to whom you present yourselves slaves to obey, you are that one's slaves whom you obey, whether of sin leading to death, or of obedience leading to righteousness?" (Rom. 6:14–16)

2

BOY PASTOR

1497—Toggenburg, Switzerland

"What? Never! You tell that boy to pack up his things and get back home immediately ... or sooner!"

Father, a sheepherder and a local amman (judge) watched the messenger turn and begin his journey back to Bern where Ulrich attended school. He looked up at the towering mountains surrounding him and thought, They can't do this to my son! He's too intelligent and talented to spend the rest of his life in a monastery. Of all my children, he has the greatest potential. Being a monk going door-to-door begging for food and money from rich and poor, young and old? No. They've learned he could make them a lot of money with his ability as a speaker, a writer, a musician.... No. My Ulrich is not going to waste his valuable life living in a monastery! The Alps seemed to echo Father's thoughts.

Ulrich soon reached the safety of home. He was greeted joyfully by his parents, one sister, and six brothers, as well as his aged grandmother. It was so good for the thirteenyear-old to spend time, especially with Grandma. He said to her, "Grandma, I've missed you telling us stories about Adam, and Job ... and Jesus."

"Well, Ulrich, those stories I've been able to glean from all the myths going around. I wish we had a Bible. then we could learn more." The printing press had been invented more than eighty years before, but the church was not interested in the truths of the Bible and kept to its own teachings and traditions.

Ulrich loved his home in the valley, but his brain and heart yearned for knowledge. So, he traveled to a different school in Basel. There he met a teacher, Professor Wittenbach, who taught Hebrew and Greek and had been led to the Scriptures. There he had learned the message of freedom and peace in Jesus. In turn, Ulrich learned the true gospel of forgiveness of sins without paying money, that the death and resurrection of Christ is the sinner's only ransom and hope.

Ulrich was soon appointed as a priest to give sermons and to lead the people. Still a teenager, but very intelligent and a talented speaker, he took his duties seriously. He began studying the Bible, comparing Scripture with Scripture, and preaching the gospel of Christ Jesus as the only hope of the world. People flocked to his meetings; many hadn't been to church for years. He believed the best way to counteract the errors of the church was to teach the truth from the Bible. He loved to teach the children.

He refused to encourage the payment of indulgences—the church's method of raising funds, teaching that if a person would pay so much, his sin would be forgiven. Also, that the sins of people who had died would be forgiven for a certain fee. In those days magnificent cathedrals were built from the sale of indulgences. Nowhere in the Bible was that teaching found.

As a result, Ulrich found himself in a lot of trouble with the leaders of the church. Along with many other unbiblical teachings that he opposed, he began to get himself into deeper difficulty, saying, "The Bible and the Bible only!" This saying became the watchword of the Protestants, the number of which was growing rapidly in every nation in Europe.

Many wars developed as a result. Thousands lost their lives by either fighting in those wars, by starving in dungeons, or by being burned to death at the stake. But when one fell, another took his place in the growth of religious liberty. Ulrich lost his life in a military battle at age forty-eight.

Someone said, "When Christ, the Son of God, had been put to death, fishermen rose up to fill His place. And now, if you destroy the preachers of the Truth, you will see glaziers, millers, potters, founders, shoemakers and tailors teaching in their stead" (S. J. Williams, *The New Reformed Pastor: Zwinglian Wisdom for Modern Ministers* [Doctoral thesis, Bethel University] (2015): 19, Spark Repository, https://1ref.us/kp01).

The Word of God is eternal—from eternity in the past to eternity in the future!

Ulrich Zwingli
1484–1532

"Therefore we also, since we are surrounded by so great a cloud of witnesses, let us lay aside every weight, and the sin which so easily ensnares us, and let us run with endurance the race that is set before us, looking unto Jesus, the author and finisher of our faith" (Heb. 12:1–2).

3

OUT OF THE MOUTH OF BABES

1520—Metz, France

Little Peter was riding his stick horse around the house when he saw his mother and her lady friends go into her bedroom and he followed them. He loved his mother so much because, well, one reason was because she would tell him stories from the Bible. How interesting and exciting they were, especially the ones about Jesus, the Son of God, and how He played with little children, took them in His arms and blessed them.

Mother's friends came and joined her in talking about the latest news of how the State Church was punishing people if they chose to believe what the Bible said instead of the church's teachings. They talked secretly in Mother's bedroom, afraid of being discovered. Peter played nearby trying to understand. Mother said with fervency, "Antichrist will soon come with great power and destroy those who have been converted at the preaching of Elias." Many times in the future he would hear those words.

Peter's family, though not rich, were distinguished for their hard work to help others in Metz. Peter's intellect amazed everyone. His uncle, a member of the college administration, agreed with Peter's mother on the importance and truth of the Scriptures and took Peter under his guiding arm. The boy learned to read quickly and easily and began to read the Bible to others, and many were won to the truth of Christ.

> *Peter's intellect amazed everyone. His uncle, a member of the college administration, agreed with Peter's mother on the importance and truth of the Scriptures and took Peter under his guiding arm.*

Most of Peter's family hoped to see him become a leader in the State Church someday. However, his genius and love for Jesus led him in another direction. He taught and preached from the Bible. But that was against the law. Other Bible teachers such as Leclerc and Chatelaine, were being arrested. The State Church had given Peter a small stipend to persuade him to work for them, but as he studied the Bible, he said to himself, "Might not the preaching of Leclerc and Chatelaine be that of Elias?"

Things became so dangerous that Peter's uncle and mother decided to move him out of Metz to Basel, Switzerland. All who listened and believed in the gospel were in danger of being hanged or burned. But the Protestant faith struggled and grew despite the shedding of blood and death. Peter stayed with it, though, and for many years supported and preached Jesus, the Bible and the Bible only!

Peter Toussaint

~1515–?

1843—Scandinavia

Another amazing thing happened in Northern Europe in the early 1840s. It was a time when Bible prophecy was being fulfilled, especially the Book of Daniel, chapters 7–12. Bible believers and scholars around the world concluded that Jesus would soon come back to earth with great power

3. OUT OF THE MOUTH OF BABES

and victory, gather His people, raise the righteous dead, and take them all back to heaven with Him. The details of Daniel's prophecy were fulfilled to the letter—except the exact date. Many who gave the message were successful and thousands decided they must repent and forsake their sins and return to God their Father.

But the clergy of the State Church opposed the exciting possibility and had the preachers of the second coming thrown into jail. But God had planned a better way to reach the people. He was pleased to send the message miraculously through little children, some only six or eight years old! They came from humble homes and possessed only average intelligence for their age. They were good children and tried to live up to what was expected of them. They were too young to be arrested.

When they stood before the people, it was evident that they had received a special portion of the Holy Spirit. They warned their hearers to put away their worldly and dishonest practices. Many who heard went home to examine the Scriptures for themselves. Even the clergy of the State Church were forced to acknowledge that God had made it all happen.

When Jesus lived on earth and the children shouted, sang, and praised Him, He said, "If these should hold their peace, the very stones would cry out!" (Luke 19:40, paraphrase). And He later said to the jealous Pharisees, "Have [you] never read, Out of the mouth of babes and sucklings Thou hast perfected praise?" (Matt. 21:16, KJV).

The message of Christ's second coming changed people's lives in 1844, although Scripture had indicated instead of coming to earth, He would transfer His work from the Holy Place in the heavenly sanctuary to the Most Holy Place on October 22, 1844, to accomplish the judgement and intercede for us. In that place He is now working to prepare all of us to enter with Him into our heavenly Home. Let's get ready!

> *"God has chosen the foolish things of the world to put to shame the wise.... Because the foolishness of God is wiser than men, and the weakness of God is stronger than men"* (1 Cor. 1:27, 25).

4
THE YOUNG AMANUENSIS

~1613—London, England

"What do you mean you've become a Christian?" Father's face had turned red with anger.

"I just want to belong to Jesus who died for me," Roger's eyes pleaded innocence.

"Jesus or not," Father retorted, "don't you know Christians are killing each other by the hundreds—by the thousands? Protestants are killing Catholics; Catholics are burning Protestants! What kind of belonging to Jesus is that?"

Father, an importer and trader of tailored goods, wanted his son to become an important administrator, but what now? "I'll tell you what I'm going to do so you will learn what's going on in the world. I'm going to see if my customer friend, Edward, will let you follow him around a little."

Sir Edward Coke was a lawyer and judge who tolerated no foolishness, even from King James I of England himself. Coke had witnessed for years the kings and queens of England executing each other over religion. Now James I had ordered a new Bible that emphasized obedience to authority but he also had laws passed in Parliament that made his simple word "the law." Coke had fought against this "divine right of kings."

In the meantime, he befriended the tailor's son and took him as his amanuensis (uh-man-yoo-EN-suhs), or secretary, to his meetings in the Star Chamber, the King's Bench, the Privy Council, to Parliament, and even to meetings with the king.

"Son," said Sir Edward one day, "I see you are keeping excellent records of what goes on in my meetings, and you are learning much. I've decided to send you to school. Will you go?"

"Oh, yes, sir, thank you, sir … but my family is…."

"Don't you worry, son; I see your potential and I take full responsibility. You know now what's going on and I believe you will do well."

So Roger went to the finest schools in England—Pembroke, Cambridge—and became qualified as a minister and administrator in the Church of England. But in the meantime, he had become a Puritan. Puritans believed the Church of England had corrupted itself by adopting unbiblical Catholic doctrines. The church had exercised stringent hold on people's personal lives and free choice. Roger's becoming a Puritan disqualified him from becoming a servant of the church.

In 1630 he finally decided to join the Puritans who went to America in 1620. In America, though, the same religious intolerance prevailed. Thus began Roger Williams' lifelong struggle to bring about freedom of conscience, separation of church and state, honesty, and respect for all humans, including Native Americans and Blacks.

He himself suffered much. He was arrested by the Massachusetts Bay Colony for his "dangerous" teachings. They did not take him immediately to prison because it was winter, and he was sick. When they finally came to get him, he had disappeared into the snowstorm. His flight of fifty-six miles by foot through a snowstorm ended when he was taken in by Indians who cared for him until spring. He then settled an area that he based on the principle of freedom of religion. Then after his enemies tried to take it away from him, he made a voyage to England to obtain a charter for the colony of Rhode Island which he founded successfully.

The principles of personal religious freedom and the wall of separation between church and state were included in the Constitution of the United States 100 years later.

Roger Williams
1603-1683

"For God has not given us a spirit of fear, but of power and of love and of a sound mind ... who has saved us and called us with a holy calling, not according to our works, but according to His own purpose and grace which was given to us in Christ Jesus before time began" (2 Tim. 1:7, 9).

5

SICKLY BODY, HEALTHY BRAIN

1626—Clermont-Ferrand, France

"Don't cry, Father. I'll help you take care of the babies," said Gilberte. Not much older than her siblings, three-year-old Blaise and the even younger toddler Jaqueline, Gilberte took on the responsibility of caring for them after the death of their mother.

Father, a judge and administrator in their hometown situated in the mountainous region of central France, held out his arms and gathered in his three motherless children. "I know you will, darling. We'll all work together and grow and still have good times like before." He cleared his throat and wiped his eyes with his sleeve. "Let's take some food and eat out in the backyard." So, all the children packed food into Mother's shopping basket and began life without her.

Time went quickly, the children grew, and Father did everything possible to provide for their needs. He even decided to homeschool his children. Blaise was not in good health; stomach problems had bothered him since age two. The doctors did the best they could, but his physical condition hindered him all his life. School at home was enjoyable, but Father did not teach him mathematics. On his own, Blaise learned math, then moved on to geometry and physics, much to his father's amazement.

Five years after Mother's death, the family moved to Paris where Father worked as a government employee but still taught his children at home. Then they found a lady to help with the family while Father was gone. Blaise spent much time in his room doing geometry and eventually joining a mathematics academy. He established geometric principles regarding planes measured with triangles and cubes.

> *Blaise spent much time in his room doing geometry and eventually joining a mathematics academy. He established geometric principles regarding planes measured with triangles and cubes.*

Then they moved to Rouen in northern France where Father became a tax collector. Blaise helped him in his office and found accounting problems with taxes caused his father many hours of agonizing work. He thought to himself, There has to be a machine that will come up with the right answers. So, at age eighteen, he built a small machine with notched dials which, when turned, could calculate mathematical problems. A few of those first calculators called "Pascalines" are still in existence in museums today.

Years later, he experimented with air pressure. His physical condition did not permit him to climb a mountain, but he sent up Gilberte's husband with a homemade barometer and he found that the air pressure decreased the higher he climbed.

More of his inventions included the roulette wheel, the wristwatch (his pocket watch attached to his wrist by a string), the hydraulic press, the syringe, and the public transport system that included carriages with many seats, a fixed route, time schedules and prices. And if no one waited at the stop, the carriage driver went on to the next stop.

Pascal is known for his amazing mathematical and geometric discoveries in his youth and for his religious faith in his mature years. From the time he was twenty-four, he could not eat solid food, only liquids. He died at age thirty-nine.

Here are some of his quotes:

"Unless we love the truth, we cannot know it" ("Blaise Pascal Quotes," AZ Quotes, https://1ref.us/kp04).

"There is a God shaped vacuum in the heart of every man which cannot be filled by any created thing, but only by God, the Creator, made known through Jesus" (Ibid.).

"We must learn our limits. We are all something, but none of us are everything" ("Blaise Pascal Quotes," Quotefancy, https://quotefancy.com/blaise-pascal-quotes).

"All of humanity's problems stem from man's inability to sit quietly in a room alone" (Ibid.).

"It's not those who write the laws that have the greatest impact on society. It's those who write the songs" (Ibid.).

"Lord, help me to do great things as though they were little, since I do them with your power; and little things as though they were great, since I do them in your name!" (Ibid.)

"The knowledge of God is very far from the love of Him" ("Blaise Pascal Quotes," Quotefancy, https://1ref.us/kp02).

"The strength of a man's virtue should not be measured by his special exertions, but by his habitual acts" ("Blaise Pascal Quotes," Quotefancy, https://1ref.us/kp03).

Blaise Pascal

1623–1662

"For by grace you have been saved through faith, and that not of yourselves; it is the gift of God, not of works, lest anyone should boast. For we are His workmanship, created in Christ Jesus for good works, which God prepared beforehand that we should walk in them" (Eph. 2:8–10).

6

GOOD NEWS TO PLANET EARTH

1801—Weilersbach, Germany

Father's friends sat with him in the living room talking. "I so look forward to Messiah's coming," said one. "Then we of Israel finally, after all these years, will be recognized by the whole world as God's chosen people."

"Yes, it has been a long time that we Jews have been ignored, mistreated, and persecuted by people who think they are better than we are," said another.

A third added, "And they spend their time fighting among themselves, even killing and burning at the stake."

Father, a rabbi for many years, said, "And all in the name of Jesus Christ, who they think is the Messiah."

Little Joseph, six years old, playing with his blocks on the floor, heard every word of the conversation. "Who was Jesus Christ?" he asked.

The men looked at him, surprised that he had heard their talk. "Oh," Father replied, "He was a carpenter who thought He was the Messiah. He never amounted to much."

But from that day, the thought of Jesus still hovered in the back of the little boy's brain.

A year later, he was talking to an aged neighbor when he boasted, as only a seven-year-old boy could, "You know, our Messiah is coming soon, and we Jewish people are going to rule the world!"

The old man replied kindly, "Dear boy, I will tell you who the real Messiah was; He was Jesus of Nazareth, whom your ancestors crucified, as they slew the prophets of old. Go home and read the fifty-third chapter of Isaiah, and you will be convinced that Jesus Christ is the Son of God." So, he went home, found Father's Bible (the Old Testament) and the Book of Isaiah. His school had taught him to read, and he had learned quickly. And here it was!

> Who has believed our message? Who has seen the Lord's hand in all this? It was the will of God that His Servant grow up like a tender plant rooted in dry ground.... There was nothing in His appearance to make us admire Him. He was despised and rejected by men ... and we took no pity on Him. He willingly bore our griefs.... He was pierced for our sins ... and by His wounds we are healed.... He was mistreated and falsely accused, yet He bore it all without saying a thing.... He was cut off from the land of the living and nailed to the wood.... He had done nothing violent, neither was deceit found in His mouth.... And though God made Him to be an offering for our sins, He will rise again and complete what God wants Him to do. (Isa. 53:1–12, CW)

He asked his father, "What does this mean?" To that, he was answered with such a stern silence that he never asked again. Instead, he would go and listen outside the churches, close enough so he could hear the sermons.

At age eleven he left home and began searching for truth for himself. In his search, he acquired a Bible and traveled to visit scholars, pastors, teachers, and theologians. In Rome he attended a Catholic college, where he was eventually expelled because he didn't agree with them on their doctrine of infallibility (that the pope could never make a mistake in doctrine).

Then he went to London and trained at Cambridge University to become a missionary and was sponsored by the London Society for Promoting Christianity Among the Jews. He also joined a Bible study group specializing in the second coming of Christ in the clouds of heaven. In London he joined the Church of England.

He had learned many different languages as a child: Hebrew, Latin, Greek. And later in his teens: Arabic, Persian, Aramaic, and Oriental languages in preparation for his missionary work.

Finally, he was able to travel and taught Bible in Egypt, the Levant (area east of the Mediterranean in the Arabian Peninsula), and to the Jews near Jerusalem. He traveled through Mesopotamia (what is now Iraq, Kuwait, Iran, Syria, and Turkey), Tiflis (the area between Europe and Russia), the Crimea, Khorasan (Persia where he was captured and made a slave but was later freed), Afghanistan, Abyssinia (Ethiopia), Yemen (southern tip of the Arabian Peninsula), and India.

The little boy who began his search for the right way, who at age eleven began his journey to all parts of planet Earth to share what he knew was true, will someday meet again the thousands of people he led to Christ.

Once he was robbed of everything he owned, including his clothes and had to hike 600 miles through the Central Asian mountains with bare feet to safety. Many times he almost starved or perished from thirst, and three times he was condemned to death.

But he never gave up. He came to the United States where he preached in Philadelphia and Baltimore, then to Washington, D.C. Speaking to all the members of Congress, he reported on the conditions of the nations and on the personal reign of Jesus Christ at His second coming.

He finally retired in a small village in England where he spent his days going over his notes and journaling, remembering all his adventures and the souls won to Christ and to Bible truth.

The little boy who began his search for the right way, who at age eleven began his journey to all parts of planet Earth to share what he knew was true, will someday meet again the thousands of people he led to Christ.

Joseph Wolff
1795-1862

"For I am not ashamed of the gospel of Christ, for it is the power of God to salvation for everyone who believes, for the Jew first and also for the Greek. For in it the righteousness of God is revealed from faith to faith; as it is written, 'The just shall live by faith'" (Rom. 1:16–17).

7

FINGER READING

1812—Coupvray, France

A scream rent the air of the harness shop. Father ran to the side of his three-year-old, who had collapsed to the floor holding his eye with both hands, blood running through his fingers. Father fell to his knees, lifted his crying son, and looked him in the punctured eye, then held him close, blood covering both of them. As he held him, he looked down and saw the small, pointed awl used for punching holes in leather. Little Louis had tried to push in the awl and it had slipped on the smooth leather. Being so little, his face was too close.

Father picked up his son and carried him into the house. They hurried him to the doctor who, after examining the eye, cleaning it up and bandaging it, murmured, "I'm afraid there's not much hope, but I'm going to contact the eye surgeon in Paris." But the new doctor also did not hold out any hope for saving Louis's eye. Even with medicine, Louis suffered agonizing pain for many weeks. Not only that, but infection set in, and the other eye began to deteriorate (called sympathetic ophthalmia). In another few months Louis had become totally blind.

One day, Mother said to her husband, "You know, I think we need to treat Louis much the same as our three older children. He's an intelligent boy, and I think he should grow up as a normal person. Let's teach him that he can be independent and choose to be happy."

Father stared at the floor a few moments thinking. "You're right. He doesn't need to grow up thinking he has to have somebody lead him around. I'll tell you what I'm going to do. I'll take my small axe and hew him out two sticks that he can take to feel walls, holes, and bumps."

"Yes!" exclaimed Mother. "Let's do it! And I'll train the other children to put away things where they belong so he won't trip. They need to learn that anyway." So, they treated Louis like a normal child. He learned to walk around the town and out to the countryside with his sticks (probably like our trekking poles). He went to school where his teachers found him anxious to learn, with a good memory, easy to get along with, and interested in everything.

By the time he was ten, his teachers felt he was an excellent candidate to enter the Royal Institute for Blind Youth in Paris, one of the first schools for blind children in the world. The school was an old, dilapidated building, but Louis enjoyed the feeling of security and friendship and the kindness of the teachers.

Enter Valentin Hauy, who was not blind himself but had given his life and talents to helping blind people. Along with heading the school, he did his best to invent a method of reading for them. He would soak heavy paper, then place it on a flat surface with copper wires bent into shapes of letters, dried, then made into books. There were three of these large, heavy books at the school. The children could feel the embossed letters and learn to read. Louis read and mastered the big books but realized the children could not learn to write.

During this time, the Napoleonic Wars were being fought across Europe. One of Napoleon's men, Charles Barbier, invented a raised dot system called "night writing" that soldiers could use to communicate with one another without a sound. Barbier realized his method could be used by blind people and sent his information, along with several sets of tools, to Louis's school.

Louis thought to himself, This is good! Much better than Hauy's method. But I believe this can be better. So, he started working on it, tirelessly improving the system. He reduced the number of raised dots from twelve to six, made columns for each letter, assigned spaces and their positions as characters. There were six spaces on the chart. All the combinations of raised dots and spaces represented sixty-four characters, including all the letters of the alphabet, accents, punctuation marks, and numbers! He worked night and day to complete his system, and by the time he was fifteen years old, his invention was completed. It took a while to be accepted, but now it's used around the world! In fact, today there are braille typewriters being used everywhere!

> *Louis thought to himself, This is good! Much better than Hauy's method. But I believe this can be better. So, he started working on it, tirelessly improving the system.*

Louis went on to become a professor at his school, teaching history, geometry, algebra, and music. As an organist, he was in demand all over France. He wrote music in braille. He is quoted as saying:

> Access to communication in the widest sense is access to knowledge, and that is vitally important for us if we [people who are blind] are not to go on being despised and patronized by condescending sighted people. We do not need pity, nor do we need to be reminded that we are vulnerable. We must be treated as equals—and communication is the way we can bring this about.

Louis Braille
1809-1852

> *"I will bring the blind by a way they did not know; I will lead them in paths they have not known; I will make darkness light before them, and crooked places straight. These things I will do for them, and not forsake them"* (Isa. 42:16).

8

SMART ALECK

1859—Edinburgh, Scotland

The two neighbor boys walked through the woods. Ben, son of the local miller, and twelve-year-old Aleck, whose dad was a speech teacher, stopped now and then to inspect different kinds of plants growing under the trees.

Aleck bent down to inspect a plant growing near a rotting log. "Look here, Ben, this plant is different. Let's see if we can find some more like it."

"All right, but what are you going to do with it?"

"I think I'll plant it at home to see if it will grow in regular garden soil instead of here where the soil has rotting wood in it. If we can find some more, I'll plant them in different kinds of soil."

"Oh!" exclaimed Ben. "Speaking of home, I'd better get back. Dad is probably looking for me to help him at the mill. Getting the husks off the grain is one of the jobs he needs me for. It's not easy work."

After leaving Ben at his house, Aleck started thinking. Maybe there's an easier way to husk wheat than doing it by hand. Why not a machine you could crank? So, within a few weeks, Ben's dad watched with delight as Ben and Aleck husked grain with a machine they had built that combined rotating paddles with sets of nail brushes. "Hey! You did it, guys! It works like a charm! This is going to save us hours and hours of work … and produce good flour for all the mothers in town to make bread … cookies … pies—oh! They are going to love you!"

"And you know something?" Mr. Herman continued. "I've got an idea. How would you boys like to have your own workshop? There's that empty shed out behind the house, and you can have fun inventing!"

"Yay!" the boys shouted. "Thanks for that idea!" And that's what they did. The grain husker operated at the mill for many years.

Aleck also loved poetry, art, and music. "I'm going to learn to play the piano," he announced one day.

"Oh, I'm so glad," responded his mother. "I'll find you a good teacher."

"Well, Mother, why don't you wait to do that, and see what I can do on my own. There are some lesson books at the music store, and I can learn from them." And he did. In time, Aleck had learned, even mastered, the piano, which gave his parents and two older brothers many hours of enjoyment singing together.

Mother, who was losing her hearing, became quieter and more self-absorbed. It was growing more difficult to talk to her, so Aleck decided he needed to teach her sign language. He also studied acoustics and learned from his dad better pronunciation, projecting his voice with much volume and expression. That way, he could make his mother understand.

Aleck's father, his uncle, and grandfather were all elocutionists. Elocution is the art of public speaking which requires proper pronunciation, grammar, and projection. His father wrote *Bell's Standard Elocutionist* which sold 250,000 copies in the United States and is still in demand today. Aleck learned his father's methods, and they both became active in training people who were deaf-mute.

After being homeschooled by his father at an early age, then going to elementary school, he started high school. After a year or so, he decided to quit. "What are you doing, young man?" exclaimed his dad.

"I'm just not interested in all that stuff they think I need to know. Biology, maybe, but all that other—no."

8. SMART ALECK

"So! Off to London you go! Your grandfather will teach you some things that will interest you. You're only fifteen, and you can't become an ignoramus!"

That year with his grandfather changed his life. Serious and interesting discussions in his granddad's study gave Aleck a love of learning all kinds of things. The older man taught the younger boy how to speak clearly and forcefully. In fact, the next year he was hired as a pupil-teacher of elocution and music back home in Scotland.

It was then that Father took Aleck and his brothers to see an automaton (a mechanical man) that could "talk." It interested the boys so much that they said, "We can do that!" After much study and experimenting, they built a head. One boy worked on the mechanical part of the mouth; Aleck built the skull and the wind source. Their dad was so pleased with their project he said, "I'm going to pay you boys for all the materials you have had to use to do this!" When the neighbors came in, they were amazed when the head said, "Mama." That gave Aleck the idea that he could make the family terrier talk. So, he taught the dog to growl in a continuous way, while he moved the dog's lips. And it worked!

> *That year with his grandfather changed his life. Serious and interesting discussions in his granddad's study gave Aleck a love of learning all kinds of things.*

Aleck then began serious work on another idea: how to make sound travel over an electric wire. By that time, he had gone to college in both Scotland and England. He had learned principles he needed for the idea. At age nineteen, after many mistakes and failures, he was able to send a message from his room to his friend's room down the hall. He wrote down everything he did through it all, which in later years, proved in court hearings that he had indeed invented the first telephone. Another ten years, in 1876, brought the telephone into practical use, despite some people's opinion that the whole idea was useless. (But today, drivers need to be careful of pedestrians crossing the street while texting on their cellphones. Hopefully you're not one of them!)

Aleck was so full of ideas to study, many of which he patented: ideas like the telegraph, photophone, phonograph, air conditioning, solar panels, hydroplanes, hydrofoils, alternative fuels, and metal detectors.

The boy who was too bored to go to high school finally let his brain convince him of all the possibilities!

Alexander Graham Bell
1847–1922

"The Lord says, 'I will teach you the way you should go; I will instruct you and advise you'" (Ps. 32:8, GNT).

9

AND A MERRY CHRISTMAS TO ALL!

1917—New York City

Sirens! Fire trucks! A cold, windy Christmas Eve in the big city. Someone had come in through their front door and the wind had blown in, hitting the lighted candles on their Christmas tree, setting the tree on fire. It spread quickly. The family had tried to put it out, but it was hopeless. The curtains were aflame, then the furniture and rugs. The fire had spread into the other rooms by the time the fire trucks arrived. The wind caught the flames and carried them to the house next door. Then to another and another. The firemen fought bravely. More fire trucks came. All through the cold, windy night they worked, the water freezing on their coats and gloves.

That Christmas Day saw homeless families looking for shelter and comfort for their broken hearts and exhausted firefighters under warm bed covers instead of spending a happy Christmas with their families. Everybody talked about the tragedy and the dangers of candles during their Christmas dinner. A few people had heard of electric Christmas lights at President Grover Cleveland's White House and at the home of the vice president of the Edison Electric Light Company before, but nobody had such things in their homes. And back in 1908, a Mr. Ralph Morris had put together a set of lights using a telephone switch board for power, but apparently nothing had come of it.

The Sadacca family, recent immigrants from Italy, talked about the big fire caused by candles. One of the boys, fifteen-year-old Albert said, "How about if we made some lights for Christmas trees like we do with our little birds?" The family ran a small novelty company and one of their items was wicker bird cages, each containing an artificial bird that was lit up from the inside by a tiny battery-operated flashlight bulb.

"Yes! That's a great idea, Albert!" Mother replied.

"We could put the bulbs on a string and sell them," Albert added.

Dad said, "The bulbs are expensive. Maybe if we put just eight on a string...."

So, they did. A few sets sold the first year but not many. The next December, Albert's brother, Leon, took the sets to Macy's and held a display. Sales picked up. He said, "People were afraid of anything with electric current, but we showed them that the doorbell-size battery was safe." And when the four brothers started painting the bulbs different colors, sales took off. In the 1920s, each bulb worked independently instead of in a series.

Several companies began making and selling the sets of lights. Then the Sadacca brothers suggested to all the companies that they merge into a trade organization. They all joined together and called it the National Outfitters Manufacturers Association (NOMA). Their success grew through the years. Then in 1934, brother Henri arranged a stock buyout. From then on, Albert served as president of the NOMA company that specialized in making and selling Christmas tree lights worldwide.

Albert continued inventing and improving his line by introducing outdoor weatherproof miniature lights, two-tone mini-lamps, connectors to attach strings together, and green sockets to match the green trees.

Now huge Christmas trees decorate city squares, shopping malls, and stadiums. Christmas trees are everywhere! Affluent homes have two trees, a big one in the front window to wish all the neighborhood a happy holiday, and a second one in the family room where the children and grownups open their gifts.

And how many Christmas tree bulbs are spreading cheer and laughter around the world? All from an idea that came from the tousled head of a fifteen-year-old boy from Italy!

Albert Sadacca
1901–1980

"You are the light of the world. A city that is set on a hill cannot be hidden.... Let your light so shine before men, that they may see your good works and glorify your Father in heaven" (Matt. 5:14, 16).

10
BEFORE YOUR TV

1920—Rigby, Idaho

Back and forth, back and forth, plowing the fields on his dad's 240-acre farm, fourteen-year-old Philo (fy'lo) kept thinking about how much he loved his new home. He had been born in his granddad's log cabin back in Utah, but recently his family had moved to this beautiful farm in Idaho. How exciting it was to find his new home wired for electricity powered by a gas generator. But it was broken, so Philo figured it out and fixed it. Then he had found an old motor that had been left by the previous tenants, so he had connected it to his mother's hand-operated washing machine.

Then he thought about other things while still behind the horse-drawn plow. I sure am enjoying all those electronic magazines found up in the attic! Boy! What a treasure! I'm learning so much. Along with the *Popular Science* magazines I'm able to buy at the drug store, and books at school, I'm learning a lot about electricity.

Back and forth, back and forth he trod on the turned-up soil. Hey! Maybe this is the way pictures could be picked up by electricity on television receivers—back and forth—only a lot faster than these horses go.

In those beginning days, television was operated with a combination of electrical and mechanical power. But why can't it all be electric? he thought. That would save a lot of work and expense. That's what I'll do—study it all through and see if there's a way ... there's got to be a way.

So, study he did, along with his schoolwork, farm work, and all those electronic and science magazines. Some weeks later he approached his chemistry teacher and said, "Mr. Tolman, would you have time some day after school to let me tell you about an idea I have?"

"Certainly, Philo, why don't you come into the lab tomorrow and tell me about it?"

So, the next day, Philo began his private presentation with his teacher by drawing a picture on the blackboard. By the time he finished, he had covered several of the lab's blackboards with schematics and illustrations.

"Wow, Philo, I believe you've got something here! This could be the answer to an all-electric television camera and receiver! You keep working on this. I'll help you all I can to find materials to build it. This is great! It will change the world!"

Years later Mr. Tolman presented his copied scheme of Philo's idea in court when a large, powerful electric company tried to get credit for Philo's invention of the all-electric television. And the court judged in favor of Philo Farnsworth.

In 1936, *Collier's* Weekly said, "One of those amazing facts of modern life that just don't seem possible—namely, electrically scanned television that seems destined to reach your home next year, was largely given to the world by a nineteen-year-old boy from Utah ... today, barely thirty years old, he is setting the specialized world of science on its ears." In 1999 *TIME* magazine included Philo Farnsworth as one of the "100 Most Important People of the Century."

Philo Farnsworth
1906–1971

"Study to show yourself approved by God, a workman who need not to be ashamed, rightly dividing the word of truth" (2 Tim. 2:15, MEV).

11

WRITING FROM THE WORD GO!

1934—Saskatoon, Saskatchewan, Canada

"But I'm scared!" exclaimed Farley, a teenager, to his dad.

Dad, a librarian, replied, "Don't be afraid. The most he can say is no. Then you can come back and work some more 'til you're better."

So, Farley picked up his small packet of papers and trudged to town to the office of the head editor of the Saskatoon Star-Phoenix. "Sir, I have some articles I've written about birds. Could you read them over and see if they're something you'd like to put in your paper?"

The editor took the papers and replied, "Just you sit here while I go into my office and read what you've got. I'll come out in a few minutes and let you know what I think."

Farley fidgeted in his chair, looking at the pictures on the wall and out the window thinking, Oh, I hope he likes them. I love to write about birds … love to write about lots of things. Oh, what if they're not good enough?

Soon the editor's office door opened. "Come in here, young man. Come and sit down." The editor closed the door and sat down at his desk. "Farley, these articles are interesting. You've written them well. I think our readers would enjoy them. There's so much to learn about birds, and in fact, all of nature. How would you like to start writing nature stories for our paper? You'll be the youngest ... how old are you?"

"I'll soon be fourteen."

"Great! You'll be the youngest columnist on our staff. And I'll pay you."

"Oh, thank you, sir! Birds and all of nature is a subject that never gets old."

With that, Farley began a career that spanned the world. He even began publishing his own nature newsletter called *Nature Lore*. And, as he grew older, he went on expeditions and published his field notes in the *Canadian Field Naturalist*.

One of the most exciting expeditions was assigned to him by the Canadian government to study the wolf population in the far north. The caribou numbers were getting smaller each year and the general opinion was that wolves were killing and eating them. So, Farley was to bring back documentation that would encourage eradicating the wolf population. So, he went up north with the barest of necessities and camped. The barren plains and mountains challenged him to work hard to find the answer. Some Eskimos befriended him, one of whom could speak English and taught him many things. One of those lessons, which was later confirmed by Farley's own experiences, was that wolves don't kill and eat caribou—or humans. They eat small animals like frogs, fish, etc. Then he found out, by experience again, that the true culprits

---

So, Farley picked up his small packet of papers and trudged to town to the office of the head editor of the Saskatoon Star-Phoenix. "Sir, I have some articles I've written about birds. Could you read them over and see if they're something you'd like to put in your paper?"

were Canadian hunters themselves who had decimated the caribou population. Farley had made friends with the wolves, even living among them, and had never been threatened. But the Canadian government, which included many of the hunters, rejected Farley's official report, and said that he had made it all up.

Another accomplishment that occupied five years of Farley's life was his World War II service as an intelligence officer. Probably his greatest achievement during that time was making an unofficial negotiation with a German general who joined him in "Operation Manna." Those food drops saved thousands of lives in the Netherlands. He became a Canadian army captain and was awarded six war medals.

During his lifetime, Farley Mowat wrote forty exciting books, mostly about nature, the sea, survival, history of the North, and his own experiences. His books have been translated into at least fifty-two languages. Some of the books he's written are *Never Cry Wolf*, *And No Birds Sang*, *The Dog Who Wouldn't Be*, *Gray Seas Under*, *The Greatest Survival Stories*, *Aftermath*, *No Man's River*, *High Latitudes*, *The Caribou of Keewatin*, *The Black Joke*, *Otherwise*, *Lost in the Barrens*, *Serpent's Coil*, *The Siberians*, and *Woman in the Mists*.

He said, "Without a function, we cease to be. So, I will write til I die" ("Farley Mowat Quotes," AZ Quotes, https://1ref.us/kp06). He also said, "Inaction will cause a man to sink into the slough of despond and vanish without a trace" (Ibid.). There are 300 acres on Cape Breton Island, owned by the Nova Scotia Nature Trust, an area now known as "Farley's Ark."

Farley Mowat
1921–2014

> *"I know how to be abased, and I know how to abound. Everywhere and in all things I have learned both to be full and to be hungry, both to abound and to suffer need. I can do all things through Christ who strengthens me"* (Phil. 4:12–13).

12

WRITTEN IN SECRET, PUBLISHED TO THE WORLD

1942—Amsterdam, Netherlands

"The Nazis are coming to our city to round up all of us Jewish people and cart us off to horrible places to either make slaves of us or to kill us," said Father.

"Can we go and hide someplace?" asked Mother. "Thousands have been killed or have died with terrible diseases—or worse yet, are being gassed to death in those terrible concentration camps."

"That insane Adolf Hitler has succeeded in convincing too many Germans that Jews are inferior to all people and should be exterminated. His motivation could be that they put Jesus to death … but that doesn't make sense. He doesn't care about Jesus. Anyway, the whole thing is crazy, and our family is in danger. I signed up for us to go to the United States, but that office has closed now and I'm sure our application has been destroyed."

"Maybe Miep and Jan Gies could help us. They are good Christian Gentiles, and we could trust them."

"Well, I'll go see them. Maybe we could hide in the big building where my business is. That's got four stories with a couple of additional buildings attached to the back. I'll go see them."

Miep, Father's secretary, had been a refugee in Amsterdam after World War I and now worked for Father. She knew what it was to be homeless and hungry. Father, Otto Frank, had a wholesale pectin and spice business, successful because those were ingredients to make and flavor sausage, a favorite food among the people there. Miep and Jan said, "Absolutely, and we'll see to it that you have food." Otto invited Herman van Pels, another employee, with his wife and son, Peter, and Dr. Fritz Pfeffer, a dentist, to join them in hiding. Along with Otto, his wife, Edith, and two daughters, Margot (fifteen) and Anne (thirteen), they all made quite a group.

In 1942, they all moved in, secretly gathering furniture, supplies, and food, eight people all living together in one of the back buildings behind the Pectacon spice company. Another employee and trusted friend came and built a bookcase to hide the entrance between the office and the stairs to the secluded living quarters. The spice business went on day by day as usual, and the inhabitants in hiding had to stay extremely quiet. The girls had to continue their studies each day. In the evenings, they could roam about the building, visit, and relax.

Just before her thirteenth birthday, Anne had received a gift of a black and red checkered autograph book. When they went into hiding, she thought to herself, This book has a lock on it. Why don't I make this into a diary? So, every day she wrote in her diary many things that happened between the eight inmates of that secret hideaway. Her own thoughts, opinions, dreams, and hopes were included. Writing down all those things seemed to ease her mind. She called her diary "Kitty." "Dear Kitty," she would write, "You will not believe what happened between Mother and Mrs. Van Pels today!" Or "Dear Kitty, That Dr. Pfeffer is a good man, but sometimes he gets a little crazy. But then, we all get a little crazy cooped up in this place. But I know it's where we should be. The Lord is with us. And our friends are seeing to it that we get food and stay healthy."

12. WRITTEN IN SECRET, PUBLISHED TO THE WORLD

Sometimes Anne and Peter, who was about the same age, would get together and talk. At first, their relationship was cool, but as time went by, they became close friends, comparing their outlook and opinions of right and wrong. Anne enjoyed talking with someone her own age.

For two years those eight people lived together with good times and hard times. They played Monopoly and other table games. Anne wrote it all down. When she ran out of space in her little book, Miep would bring her more writing paper.

The outside world was in worse turmoil: battles in Europe and in the East, ships sinking, airplanes fighting and crashing, bombs falling, thousands of lives lost, the German police (Gestapo) gathering in all the Jews and sending them off to death.

And then on August 4, 1944, the Gestapo got word that there were eight Jews hiding in one of the back buildings of the Pectacon spice shop. How they were informed, nobody since has been able to identify the culprit for sure. But in they came, crashing and jamming, roughly dragging all of them downstairs into trucks and then onto a train that took them to different concentration camps. Anne and Margot were allowed to stay together, but they both soon became sick with typhus from which they never recovered.

After the war, it was found that Otto was the only one of the eight who survived. He traveled far and near searching for his family and friends but found that they all had perished in the Holocaust.

Then Otto went back to the Pectacon company where Miep still worked. "Is there anything left of my life?" he asked.

Miep answered, "Yes, Mr. Frank. Among the things scattered on the floor up there, we found Anne's papers and diary. I have kept them, and you can have them."

"Oh, thank God! And thank you, Miep. I will treasure them as long as I live!" And do you know what Otto did with that diary? He thought to himself, Anne's greatest wish was to become a journalist, a professional writer. If I have her diary published as a book, that will help people understand all we have gone through. So that's what he did.

The book *The Diary of a Young Girl* was translated from the original Dutch into English and published in 1952. It has since been translated into more than seventy languages around the world and made into a film!

As President Bill Clinton said in her memory:

> Now, more than seventy years since the first publication of her diary, Anne Frank endures as one of the great messengers of our common humanity. Through her courage, her hope, and her unshakable faith in the goodness of people—despite the grave injustices visited upon her and her family throughout her brief life—she continues to give a voice and a face to six million Jews who lost their lives in the Holocaust. Her short life left a long legacy, touching and inspiring generation after generation of people she never met. ("Dedication of Anne Frank Tree," Clinton Presidential Center, Little Rock, AR, Oct. 2, 2015)

Anne Frank
1929–1945

"O enemy, destructions are finished forever! And you have destroyed cities; even their memory has perished. But the LORD shall endure forever.... He shall judge the world in righteousness.... The LORD also will be a refuge for the oppressed, a refuge in times of trouble. And those who know Your name will put their trust in You; for You, LORD, have not forsaken those who seek You" (Ps. 9:6–10).

13

I LOVE THE FLAG!

1957—Lancaster, Ohio

"Alright, class, since we've been talking about Alaska and Hawaii maybe joining the United States sometime soon, what changes will take place?" asked the high school American history teacher, Mr. Stanley Pratt.

"I know," said one student, raising his hand. "The number of senators and representatives will increase in Congress."

"That's right," replied the teacher. "What else?"

Another hand shot up. "The cost of sending mail."

"True. What else?"

Another hand up. "The flag will change."

"That's right!" said Mr. Pratt. "I'll tell you what I'm thinking. You all like doing art. Why don't you each design a new flag that reflects the new states. You know the flag has changed more than two dozen times since the first one back in 1777. Why don't you come up with some ideas of your own?"

The students looked at each other, their faces lighting up with new thoughts and ideas. Artwork! Fun for a change! One student, Bob, thought on his way home, I know what I can do! Maybe Mom will help me.

But when Mom, an experienced seamstress, learned of his plan, she said, "No, son, I'll supply you with material and equipment, and you can use my sewing machine, but you'll have to do it yourself."

"Can I use that flag that somebody gave us and cut it up?"

"Well, I guess so since it won't be of any use soon anyway. Go ahead."

So, Bob took the family flag and carefully, carefully cut out each star. Mother supplied some more white material for the two extra stars, also a square of blue. Then Bob marked, arranged, and carefully pinned the fifty stars in alternating rows onto the blue.

"You know, son, you've never used a sewing machine before. You'd better practice before you sew on your flag," Mother suggested, getting him some older fabric. Then Bob sat down and began working the treadle, which didn't always do what he wanted. She showed him how to turn directions on his stitching by being certain the needle was down when he turned the material.

Well, it took him about twelve hours to sew on all the stars, plus sewing the blue field of stars onto the stripes of the family flag.

"Good job!" exclaimed his parents. And Bob proudly carried his flag to the next history class. But when the grades came out, he only got a B minus! He groaned. All that hard work!

Mr. Pratt explained, "Bob, I was hoping you'd come up with something more original."

"But, sir! It's American! Red, white, and blue! Courage, purity, and justice! And, and ... stability!"

Mr. Pratt looked at Bob's flag. "I'll tell you what, Bob, if the government adopts your flag, I'll give you an A."

"It's a deal!" replied Bob.

That evening, Dad said, "You know, Bob, maybe Walter Moeller would be the one who could help you." Moeller was an Ohio Congressman in Washington, D.C.

Well, the rest is history. Robert Heft's flag design was officially chosen as the twenty-seventh United States flag on July 4th, 1960. And Bob got his A!

He eventually became mayor of an Ohio city and also spent much of his time as a motivational speaker, encouraging young and old to take courage and keep going in spite of opposition and troubled circumstances.

13. I LOVE THE FLAG!

Robert G. Heft
1942–2009

"Be strong and of good courage; do not be afraid, nor be dismayed, for the LORD your God is with you wherever you go" (Josh. 1:9).

14
LET THERE BE LIGHT

1972—Toledo, Ohio

"If only I could see!" exclaimed ten-year-old Becky as she sat in the car waiting for Mother in the grocery store. The papers in her lap had become almost invisible as it grew darker and darker outside. She opened the glove compartment but found no flashlight. She thought, If I open the door, the whole inside will light up. Anyway, Mother says to keep the doors locked 'til she comes back. There are lightning bugs out now, but there's not enough. Just then Mother came back and they went home.

For several days Becky thought about how to write in the dark. There must be some way to make my paper light up. There are fluorescent lights. Could I make other things fluorescent? She went out to the living room where Dad was reading the newspaper. "Dad, could I make my paper light up like a fluorescent light?"

He put down his paper and replied, "I don't think that's what you want, honey. Fluorescent needs a constant power source. Why don't you go get one of your Frisbees and maybe we can figure out something else."

She ran to her toybox and brought a Frisbee. Dad said, "Okay, now turn off the lights."

"Oh! They're shining in the dark!"

"Yes, that's because they're painted with phosphorescent paint. It needs only a few minutes of light then it will shine in the dark for up to maybe a half hour or more."

So, the next day Dad and Becky went to the hardware store and bought some phosphorescent paint. Back home, Becky painted some writing paper. Writing on that didn't work. Then she put another sheet on top of it and she could see to write and draw pictures on that. In the dark! "Dad! Mom! It works! I put a sheet of paper on the painted sheet, and it shines through, and I can see to write on it!"

They both came in to see it and Dad said, "You know, kid, I think you have invented a useful thing! A lot of people would like something like this in their work."

"I could call it my Glow Sheet!"

"We're going to do something about this!" Dad exclaimed. And he did. Being a patent lawyer, he immediately applied for a United States patent on Becky's discovery. By the time she turned twelve, her invention held a legal patent number! She is the youngest girl to hold a US patent!

But she didn't stop there. She came up with painting clipboards, painting lines to guarantee a neat looking document, and other improvements. Before she was done, she had accumulated nine more patents, and started her own company, The B.J. Products, Toledo, Ohio.

The *New York Times* publicized her inventions, and everybody decided they needed at least one! Hospitals used them for doctors and nurses who need them to take notes without turning on the patients' lights. Emergency medical technicians began using them in ambulances. Sailors out on the high seas could write in the dark without alerting the enemy. Photographers used them in their darkrooms. Critics could take notes in darkened theaters. Astronauts could use them in orbit while their electric system recharged. And students sometimes need to write their assignments in the dark. A ten-year-old girl needs to write in a darkened car. That's how inventions come to be!

Rebecca Schroeder
1962–

"In the beginning God created the heavens and the earth. The earth was without form, and void; and darkness was on the face of the deep.... Then God said, 'Let there be light'; and there was light. And God saw the light, that it was good; and God divided the light from the darkness. God called the light Day, and the darkness He called Night. So the evening and the morning were the first day" (Gen. 1:1–5).

15

PRECIOUS GARBAGE

1982—Cateura, Paraguay

Thirteen-year-old Favio, gifted with the talent of music, began to think how he could give music lessons to his friends and the younger children in his neighborhood and make a little money. He did well, but then his family moved from Cateura to Carapegua. There he decided to teach music in his new hometown. After teaching his students the basics, he began to teach them to play instruments. Their parents were especially pleased when he organized a small orchestra.

When he grew older, he became qualified for a position as an environmental consultant, which took him back to his hometown, Cateura. It's more than a town; it's a city of 40,000 located in a swampland between the capital city of Asuncion and the Paraguay River. One and a half tons of garbage are brought by dump trucks to Cateura every day, and the workers, called recyclers or gancheros, make their living by sorting through the trash and selling plastic bottles and other reusable items. With the few pesos they make, they must feed their families. The hot sun, the flies, rodents, mosquitos, and stench must be accepted by the men and women who work there. They live in shacks with dirt floors, and their children play on the mountains of trash. Poverty, disease, and crime are considered normal.

Favio was hired to train the gancheros how to select the best and most saleable items. On weekends, he would return to his clean, quiet home in Carapegua, where he could practice music with his youth orchestra. Sometimes they would give concerts in neighboring cities. And when he took his orchestra to his hometown, Cateura, the people loved it. They exclaimed, "Favio! Our kids need something like this! They are spending too much time on the trash mounds. They need something like this! Could you teach them music? Please, Favio!"

So, Favio went home and began to think. Yes, those kids don't have much of a future except to collect trash like their parents. Music would excite them. It would give them a chance to dream. If you're born in the wrong place, you don't have a right to dream. When I was young, music was the first thing that gave me a sense of purpose.

"Yes! I'll do it!" he exclaimed out loud. So, he started offering free music lessons to the children of the Cateura gancheros. And what a response!

But ... but ... where am I going to get instruments? Why, they could never afford an instrument. A violin is worth more than the house they live in. And even if they had one, their parents would be tempted to sell it. What am I going to do? Have I got myself into something I can't handle?

Almost as an answer to prayer, Favio met Nicolas "Cola" Gomez, and it changed his life. Cola was a rubbish picker that had some experience as a carpenter. Favio and Cola started talking and came up with the idea of making the instruments. "I could take some oven trays home with me," suggested Cola, "and use my electric saw to shape the metal like a violin."

"You got it, Cola!" exclaimed Favio. "Let's do it! The kids can have their own instruments at home, and their parents won't be tempted to sell them because they aren't worth anything!"

So, Favio and Cola began turning old oven trays into violins, water pipes into clarinets, flutes, and saxophones, oil drums into cellos, and all kinds of garbage into trumpets and trombones! And they made drums using X-rays for drumheads!

Soon there were thirty children, each with their own instrument. Favio provided lesson sheets and taught them how to play. His regime was a tough one, though, because he required each student to practice two hours a day! But they loved it. "It's fun to learn to play music," they said. "Maybe we can have an orchestra too!"

And they did. Favio didn't work as an environmental consultant anymore and had another job in Carapegua, but he would come to Cateura once a week to organize and conduct the children's orchestra. He would say, "You're doing great, guys. Keep it up. Here's another piece of music to work on. Maybe, if you do well, we'll soon be playing concerts in other towns!"

It wasn't long before that dream came true. No one had to play on the garbage mounds; they stayed home, learning new music and how to count whole notes, quarter, and eighth notes.

When word reached the local radio station, the public's enthusiasm knew no bounds. Hundreds of people came to their concerts. So it was that the Landfill Harmonic Orchestra came to the attention of the world. Gancheros' children traveled all over Latin America to Europe and to North America and played sold-out concerts in huge arenas, presenting classical music, such as Pachelbel's *Canon*.

The world and their dreams expanded. "Maybe we can be more than garbage pickers after all!" they said to each other. And, as Favio says, "Having nothing is not an excuse for doing nothing" ("'Recycled Orchestra' Turns Trash into Music," The Christian Broadcasting Network, https://1ref.us/kp07).

Favio Chavez
1969–

"For here we have no continuing city, but we seek the one to come"
(Heb. 13:14).

16

CHILD SLAVES

1987—Muridke, Islamic Republic of Pakistan, near Lahore in Punjab

Father needed money. He had left his Christian family several months before, leaving his wife to raise the children and make a living as a cleaning lady. He came home one day. The two oldest girls were delighted to see him. "Father! Have you come home to us?"

"No, I've come to take Iqbal." He picked up little brother and left without another word. The girls hoped he would come back, but he didn't. Instead, he took Iqbal to a carpet factory and loaned him out for 600 rupees. The loan was to be paid off by Iqbal's labor, including an interest rate unknown to Father, expenses that included a year's training without pay, expenses, tools, food, and fines for mistakes Iqbal made.

The little four-year-old boy cried the first night until he couldn't cry any more. "Mama!" he sobbed. "I want my Mama!" The other children tried to comfort him, but they were too tired after their fourteen-hour workday. They had been given little to eat and besides, they had been through it all.

Like them, he was taught how to tie strong strings to make carpets. But you know how a four-year-old would like to work even an hour at the same job in the same place—let alone fourteen hours. He would get off his stool and wander around, trying to find a friend who would play with him, then a big man would grab him, get him back to his place and shout, "Get to work, you little beggar, or you'll get more of the same or worse!" Which he did. Beatings didn't help. The boy tried to escape, and when that didn't work, he would refuse to work and run around the factory until he was caught and beaten again. Finally, Iqbal was chained to his loom. He got more beatings until he lost all hope and in silence tied knots and made carpets.

One American professor has said, "Large numbers of Christians in the Punjab and Sindh area, in particular, are trapped in bonded labor or slavery in work like brick kilns and carpet weaving."

Father's inability to pay back the money with Iqbal's labor increased as the weeks and months—and years—went by. What was owed amounted to 30,000 rupees. Then something happened. When Iqbal turned ten, he learned that bonded labor had been declared illegal by the Supreme Court of Pakistan. After much silent planning in his mind, one night he escaped. Running in the dark, he made his way to the police station. Bursting through the front door and breathing like an old man, he said, "I've come to report Ashad at the carpet factory. He's got a lot of kids like me working as slaves!"

> *After much silent planning in his mind, one night he escaped. Running in the dark, he made his way to the police station. Bursting through the front door and breathing like an old man, he said, "I've come to report Ashad at the carpet factory. He's got a lot of kids like me working as slaves!"*

"Well!" replied the policeman. "That's no good. Come, show us where we can find him."

So, he showed them where Ashad was. Then they grabbed Iqbal, dragged him in and announced, "We have one of your boys."

"Well! Iqbal, it's you!"

The policeman said, "We've got to get back."

Ashad took out several rupees from his pocket and handed them to the policeman. "Finder's fee. Thanks, boys."

Then Iqbal escaped a second time, but this time he knew a better place to go. He went to the home of Mr. Kahn, the head of the Bonded Laborer Liberation Front (BLLF), where he was hidden, fed, and protected. He had, at ten years old, the height and weight of a six-year-old. As soon as he was well, they started teaching him. "Oh, I'm so glad to go to school!" he exclaimed. He learned all the fundamentals and finished the four-year course in two years.

During that time, and with the help of Mr. Kahn and the Bonded Laborer Liberation Front, Iqbal helped 3,000 other children to escape slavery. He traveled the world speaking against child slavery. In 1994, while in Boston, he received the Reebok Human Rights Award and with it, $50,000 to use in his work. In his acceptance speech he said:

> I am one of those millions of children who are suffering in Pakistan through bonded labour and child labour, but I am lucky that due to the efforts of Bonded Labour Liberation Front, I go out in freedom I am standing in front of you here today. After my freedom, I joined BLLF School and I am studying in that school now. For us slave children, Ehsan Ullah Khan and BLLF have done the same work that Abraham Lincoln did for the slaves of America. Today, you are free and I am free too! ("Iqbal Masih," Wikipedia, https://1ref.us/kp08)

He attended several international conferences where he impressed many people with his eloquent style, denouncing child slavery in Pakistan and in other countries. As a Christian, Iqbal hoped to become a lawyer who could do away with child slavery.

But that never happened. One day, as he was cycling in his hometown with his friends, someone from the "carpet mafia" with a shotgun put a violent end to Iqbal's life. The shooter was caught, but in such a corrupt society, who knows whether he was punished or not? Iqbal's funeral was attended by approximately 800 mourners. The next week, there arose a big public protest by 3,000 people, half of whom were children under twelve, looking to end child slavery.

The rich people owning the carpet businesses responded to declining sales by hiring the Pakistan Federal Investigation Agency to brutally harass and arrest anyone working for the Bonded Laborer Liberation Front. The press conducted a smear campaign against the BLLF, saying the children were receiving high wages under pleasant conditions.

In 2009 the United States Congress began giving an annual award in Iqbal's name to activists fighting to end child labor.

Iqbal Masih
1983-1995

> *"Then a dispute arose among them [the disciples] as to which of them would be greatest. And Jesus, perceiving the thought of their heart, took a little child and set him by Him, and said to them, 'Whoever receives this little child in My name receives Me; and whoever receives Me receives Him who sent Me. For he who is least among you all will be great'"* (Luke 9:46–48).

17

THE INVISIBLE VIDEO TAPE

1994—Towson, Maryland (near Baltimore)

Everybody was crying. Dad, a state trooper, had announced to Mother the day before that he was leaving and wanted a divorce. Mother told her three children about it the next day. The four of them clung to one another and cried because they all loved Dad so much. How could they go on? How could they go to school? Mom was principal of another school; Michael, nine years old, was in sixth grade, and he had two older sisters. But go on they must, no matter how they felt.

Michael couldn't think. His broken heart pained so much he couldn't hear what was going on in class. Day after day he tried, but comfort just wouldn't come. He would look out the window and at the walls. And the blackboard just seemed too black. He would fidget and interrupt the class. After a few weeks, his teacher suggested he be taken to the doctor. Michael had always been super active and had been swimming since he was seven to work his energy off a bit, but now it wasn't enough. Nothing worked. The doctor diagnosed him as having ADHD (attention deficit hyperactivity disorder) and prescribed a child's dose of medicine. It helped a little, and slowly he became calmer. He began to enjoy his swimming again.

In fact, he began competing at swim meets, and by the time he was ten, he had won the national record in his age group with the 100-meter butterfly! Mother was so pleased at his progress that she said one day, "Michael, I'm so proud of you. How would you like to join the Aquatic Club in Baltimore so you can get more training?"

"Oh! Would I ever!"

"All right. I'll take you over there, and we'll see what you can do."

Bob Bowman, the coach at the club, had met Michael and knew the boy had just the right physique to excel as a swimmer—a long torso, shorter legs (which offer less drag in the water), long arms, and large hands. But Michael was still stressed and emotional. Coach knew he had to get him to calm down and relax. So, he went to the store and bought a book and gave it to Michael's mother, telling her to read it to Michael every night at bedtime. It was a book of exercises to help him relax. "Tighten your right hand into a fist, then open it and relax it." Then he learned to tighten and relax his feet and legs and other parts of his body until he fell asleep. And it worked.

Michael began to have a passion for swimming. The experts said that all elite athletes had this obsession for their sport. Coach Bowman taught him to establish a routine of all that needed to be done in his training each day. When he finished a day's practice, Bowman would say, "Now, go over in your mind all your moves while swimming—like a videotape in your head. Go through a race and imagine every move—what you see, what you feel until you've won the race. That will be your 'video tape.' Go through it when you wake up in the morning and again before you go to sleep at night. You'll be surprised at how easy it is, and you'll get stronger and faster. Recordings of fast music in your earphones will help also."

The mental visualization worked! Those two "keystone habits"—visualization and relaxation—helped Michael to begin winning big. Before each race he would mentally go through his "video tape." And these small mental "wins" soon became a reality!

17. THE INVISIBLE VIDEO TAPE

When Coach Bowman was transferred to another city or college, Michael followed him and continued his training. His usual routine was the following:

1. Before entering the water, stretch and exercise the arms

2. Do the same with the back and all the way down to the ankles

Then in the pool:
3. 800 meters of mixed styles (a meter is almost forty inches)

4. 600 meters of kicking

5. 400 meters of pulling a buoy between his legs

6. 200 meters of stroke drills

Then outside:
7. Sprint twenty-five meters several times to elevate the heart rate

This routine took forty-five minutes.

At age fifteen, Michael became the youngest male to make an Olympic team in sixty-eight years. He became the most successful swimmer in

Olympic history, winning twenty-eight medals—twenty-three of them gold medals. In addition, he has won eighty-two medals in international competitions. He is widely regarded as the greatest swimmer of all time, as well as one of the greatest athletes of all time.

He said, "The only reason I ever got in the water was my mom wanted me to just learn how to swim" (Kiran Rao, "'It's a fact'—Michael Phelps reiterates his quote on success," https://1ref.us/kp09).

Michael Phelps
1985–

"For as he thinks in his heart, so is he" (Prov. 23:7).

18

THE WATER BOY

1997—Kemptville, Ontario, Canada

Ryan sat fidgeting in his first-grade class when the teacher, Mrs. Prest, suddenly caught his attention. "You know, there are children in Africa who are dying because they don't have clean water to drink."

"You mean they have to drink dirty water?" asked one of the students.

"They don't have water at all in some places. Their mothers have to go sometimes for miles with waterpots on their heads to the nearest spring where there might be wild creatures, even snakes."

Another said, "My mom would never go. She'd send Dad."

The teacher replied, "In most of Africa, men think it's below their dignity to fetch water. If by some circumstance, a man has to do it, he'll go in the night so no one will see him. Still, there's not enough water for everybody."

"Where does our water come from?" asked another.

"Out of the faucet!" answered a boy, causing snickers around the room. But it was a serious question.

Six-year-old Ryan sat thinking as Mrs. Prest explained the process by which cities obtain and store water and how people out in rural areas have wells that are dug deep into the ground.

"Well, if people here get water out of the ground, why can't Africans do it?"

"Because it costs lots of money and the right kind of equipment to dig wells, which the Africans don't have."

He thought, Well, we better help them! He remembered how it felt to be thirsty. There's got to be a way! On his way home, he kept thinking, I've got to do something to help those people. But I haven't got any money ... maybe I could get some ... could earn some ... maybe—

"Hey, Mom!" he shouted coming through the front door, "Can I earn some money?"

"What's that?" asked Mother coming out from the kitchen.

Ryan explained what he had learned. "Well," Mother said, "You can work here at home."

"And would you pay me?"

"Certainly. You can save what you earn and send it to a company that can drill wells in Africa."

"Yay! When can I start?"

"Well, there's dirty dishes in the sink. Do you want to start there? I'll pay you a quarter if you wash and dry them and put them away."

"Okay!" he said, throwing off his sweater and pushing up his sleeves. All kinds of jobs around home, inside and out, awaited him, and he began putting nickels, dimes, and quarters into a glass jar. It took him four months to earn seventy dollars. Then when he found out that was not enough money, he kept working at chores and also raising funds from neighbors, churches, and local organizations, such as the Rotary Club. Within twelve months he had raised $2,000, the cost of drilling a well! He sent the money to the nonprofit charity in Canada called WaterCan that provides clean water to poor countries.

They drilled Ryan's first well in northern Uganda near a public school. When he turned eight years old, the Canadian Development Agency heard of his project and offered to match two dollars for every dollar he could raise. That totaled $61,000! As a result, he started Ryan's Well Foundation, a Canadian registered charity to build wells in Africa and to educate the children there how to stay clean and healthy.

When Ryan was nine years old, he traveled to Uganda to see his first well. He met the workers who maintained the well and the students at the school nearby. Among them was Jimmy Akana, whose parents had disappeared during a recent civil war and now lived with his aunt. Jimmy had been in the habit of awaking each midnight, getting up, and hiking five miles to fetch water. In fact, he would make three round trips for water before school started the next morning! Jimmy and Ryan became pen pals. Then Jimmy was kidnapped by a rebel group but escaped and went to live with an aid worker. Eventually Ryan's parents brought Jimmy to Canada, adopted him, and he became a Canadian citizen. The two brothers graduated from high school together.

Going to college in Nova Scotia, Ryan majored in International Development and Political Science and graduated in 2013. Ryan's Well Foundation has been instrumental in building more than 1,000 wells around the world. He has received many awards and still keeps working worldwide, with the help of many organizations, to make life bearable for thousands of poor people.

He has said, "The world is like a great big jigsaw puzzle, and we all have to figure out where our puzzle piece fits in. I figure my piece fits with clean water. I just hope everyone else finds where their puzzle piece fits too!" (adapted from "Ryan Hreljac," Haiku Deck, https://1ref.us/kp10). Those few coins in a glass jar were multiplied thousands of times as a result of Ryan's willingness to do the dishes!

Ryan Hreljac

1991–

"Blessed is he who considers the poor. The LORD will deliver him in time of trouble. The LORD will preserve him and keep him alive, and he will be blessed on the earth" (Ps. 41:1–2).

19

THE ELECTRONIC BRAIN

2006—Freetown, Sierra Leone, West Africa

Mother came through the front door after her work in the city to find her youngest son sitting on the floor cluttered with trash. "Kelvin! What are you doing with all this mess?"

"I'm trying to build some kind of a light, so we can see at night," replied her tenyear-old, the youngest of her five children.

"But why all these old radios, cables, and … and …?"

"Well, I picked it all up at the dump, and maybe I can do something with it."

Mother sighed. "All right, son, do your best, but try to keep things out of the way so we can get through the living room."

Sierra Leone ("Mountain of the Lion") is a small country on the Pacific coast of West Africa. There had been a brutal civil war over whether the country would be ruled by one political party or by more than one. Finally, the multiparty system prevailed but not until thousands of lives had been lost. Sierra Leone is a republic and part of the British Commonwealth where Elizabeth II served as their queen. But it is an independent country where religion and government are separated. Muslims make up about 75% and Christians 21% of the population. English is spoken by the educated but 99% speak Krio. Schools struggle to keep going, and more than half the population is twenty-five years old or younger.

Kelvin was determined to help his family and neighbors get some light. Since the electricity would come on only once a week, he worked and studied through the problem and came up with a light made of soda, acid, and metal in a tin cup wrapped in tape. The neighbors were grateful. "Hey, Kelvin, thanks for giving us light for our dark nights!"

Kelvin visited the city dumpsites regularly after school. He figured out how to put together pieces and parts, and eventually, made a radio transmitter, a mechanical generator, a sound amplifier, a microphone receiver, and a three-channel mixer! Then he decided, "Maybe, just maybe, I could set up a radio station! It might not go much farther than our neighborhood, but wouldn't it be fun!" So, his radio station came to be called "DJ Focus."

Word got out to the African YouTube channel THNKR, which took Kelvin's story, resulting in thousands learning of his achievements. One such spectator, David Sengeh, another young man from Sierra Leone, a graduate from MIT (Massachusetts Institute of Technology), invited Kelvin, then sixteen years old, to go to Massachusetts with him, where Kelvin became the youngest person to participate in the Visiting Practitioners Program at MIT, a program that helps inventors go into business with their products.

During the same trip, David took him to New York City, where Kelvin appeared at the World Makers Faire 2012 on a panel called Meet the Young Makers.

"It's an opportunity for him to create the future that he wants to live in," said Sengeh, now a Senior Fellow at TED (Technology, Education and Discovery).

Since then, Kelvin has appeared on TEDxTeen, given a lecture at Harvard, and signed a contract with a Canadian WIFI company to develop solar inventions.

On the side, Kelvin became an honorary member of Emergency USA, a nonprofit that provides medical care for those affected by war and poverty. Now he's living in Ontario, Canada, pursuing his studies in electronics and business.

Even though he still gets homesick for his family back in Africa, he carries on with the same determination he had scavenging the dumpsites at age ten! Kelvin says, "Creativity is universal and can be found in places where one does not expect to find it. Perseverance and passion are essential to nurturing that creative ability."

Kelvin Doe
1996–

"Trust in the LORD, and do good; dwell in the land, and feed on His faithfulness. Delight yourself also in the LORD, and He shall give you the desires of your heart" (Ps. 37:3–4).

20

FIRSTHAND

2010—Mancos, Colorado

Easton sat on the floor in his bedroom with all the parts of a microwave oven scattered around him. I've got to find out how this works, he thought to himself. Just then the bedroom door opened and there was Dad with a fire extinguisher, which he quietly brought in, laid on the floor, and went back out without a word. Easton got the message: be careful what you're doing! He loved taking things apart and learning how they work. At ten years old, he built a radio-controlled car out of Legos and a small motor.

Then he decided to go online and learn about robotics (the study of the design, building, operation, and application of robots). School was okay, but he was more interested in coming up with new inventions. He went on YouTube, talked with people on Skype, and decided to see if he could make a robotic hand. Let's see ... Oh! I could use my Legos, some tubing. Where will I get tubing? Oh, the hospital would have that. Then fasten it all together with Dad's fishing wire. Then I could put the whole thing in a glove. And that's what he did. The eighth-grade science fair would be coming up soon, so he entered his artificial hand in the fair. He came in second, which inspired him to improve his invention so it could move.

So, learning how to use 3D printing from a professor nearby, he made an arm and connected it to the hand. He learned about sensors, how they can be put on an upper arm or leg and detect the brain's feeling pain or wanting to move fingers or toes. Electricity was needed, so he acquired small batteries for the project. By now, he was ready to enter the Colorado State Science Fair where he won third prize. After more research and rebuilding, he entered the Engineering Section of the International Science Fair. While there, he met a little girl who took an unusual interest in his display, moving the fingers, and feeling the arm. Then he saw that she was wearing an artificial arm herself.

The girl's mother asked, "How much did it cost you to build this?"

"Oh, about $200," he replied.

The mother groaned, "This artificial arm cost us $80,000!"

"You mean...?"

"Yes! And if you can make more of these, you're in business! And we'll be your first customers! Think of all the millions of people around the world who need artificial limbs—wounded veterans, people who've had to have their hands or arms amputated, and I've heard even of some who've had their arms cut off by the cruelty of enemies!" That day launched Easton's life mission.

He went home and buried himself in study and research. He began working with scientists, such as Microsoft engineers at the Advanced Prototyping Center. He said, "We're going to keep working to make this better and better."

After partnering with Microsoft, his first successful robotic arm was given to Momo, a nine-year-old Oriental girl, who found she could swim as fast as her friends with her new arm.

Now Easton has become a robotic engineer and a businessman. At age seventeen, he worked for NASA (National Aeronautics and Space Administration) in developing the "robonaut." He has founded his own company called Unlimited Tomorrow. He uses 3D printing, 3D scanning, Bluetooth, and artificial intelligence to make and supply thousands of artificial limbs to people around the world. In fact, he has offered an "open source" business, where people can make their own artificial limbs in their own home for free! He has earned many awards and achieved much as a teenager.

1. Second place at the Intel International Science and Engineering Fair

2. Team member, Robonaut Project, NASA

3. Founder of Unlimited Tomorrow

4. Third place, Colorado Science Fair

5. Forbes 30 Under 30

6. Active in STEM (Science, Technology, Engineering, and Mathematics), a program to develop interest and training of young students

7. Appeared on TED (Technology, Entertainment and Design)

He is quoted as advising young people interested in the STEM organization:

> Explore your curiosity. This is the driving force of what made me start this and to continue moving forward. In today's world, there are vast amounts of resources at your fingertips. Use these resources to explore and find your passion. There is no excuse not to do what you love.
>
> I taught myself programming, electronics, and mechanics from the internet, YouTube, online forums, Skyping people around the world, and trial and error.
>
> Don't be afraid to stray away from the 'normal path.' There are so many ways in today's world to continue learning to do what you love. There's a lot of things that put you on a conventional path, but don't let others decide your future. Be bold and stay curious. ("This alum prints prosthetics of the future," Society for Science, https://1ref.us/kp11).

Easton LaChappelle
1996–

"The LORD has done great things for us, and we are glad" (Ps. 126:3).

21

THE LITTLE RED WAGON

2004—Tampa, Florida

Hurricane Charlie sped up to 150 miles an hour and destroyed thousands of homes across the whole region from Africa to the eastern seaboard of America, leaving trees uprooted, electric wires downed, debris, and many thousands of people homeless, injured, hungry, without water, and dying.

Seven-year-old Zach, who lived with his mother and older sister, had some damage to their home but not as bad as others around the State of Florida. His dad had lost his life in a motorcycle accident a few years before.

"What can I do to help all these people?" he asked his mother, a real estate agent.

"Well, son, the problem is too big to help everybody. Do you have any ideas? What are the simple needs that people don't have?"

"They need food and water."

"Yes. How about water?"

"Well, we still have water coming out of our faucets." So, Zach began collecting bottles and jars, cleaning and filling them with water, and delivered them in his little red wagon. His mother helped collect more containers and arranged for a man to deliver the containers of water in his pickup truck. Zach filled the truck with water twenty-seven times and relieved the needs of hundreds of hurricane victims, among whom were many homeless children.

"Hey, Mom!" he shouted, coming in the back door one day. "I heard about a bunch of people who are helping called 'Start Up for Kids' and I've joined them! I'm going to help deliver stuff in my wagon to homeless kids!"

Mother replied, "That's great, son. And why don't you start an organization—a nonprofit—to collect funds for buying things they need?"

"Yeah, I can use my wagon!"

So, that's how The Little Red Wagon Foundation came to be. He helped collect backpacks that he filled with donated snacks, toys, soap, shampoo, etc. He called them "Zachpaks." Before he was finished, he had distributed 10,000 Zachpaks to homeless children!

How did he get all that done and still go to school? Well, he's been a hard worker. And with God's help, he has grown strong and active. Even at three years old, he started Taekwondo training (junior class) and after several years he earned his black belt. He went to school by Internet through the K-12 Virtual Instruction Program. During that time, he decided to help homeless children. It is estimated that there are at least 1.3 million homeless children in the United States alone—not counting those worldwide!

Zach says, "These kids don't have a home; they don't have a safe place to sleep at night. They're out on the streets, not because they want to be, but because it's out of their control."

When he was eight, he hosted Christmas parties and gave gifts to homeless children after Hurricane Katrina in New Orleans, Louisiana, in 2005 that caused 1,800 deaths and $125,000,000,000 in damages. At age ten he organized "24 Hours" where high school students each paid twenty-four dollars and lived for twenty-four hours in a cardboard box. He did this for seven years. From 2007–2009, he walked "From My House to the White House" raising funds for homeless children. His mother and sister helped him along the way.

When Zach was twelve years old, he walked from Tampa, Florida, to Los Angeles, California, distributing gift cards to homeless children. Many news organizations, including NBC News, kept tabs on him. His mother and sister helped take care of him. He is the youngest person to walk from the East Coast to the West Coast—2,478 miles!

Michael Guillen, CEO of the Philanthropy Project said, "He's sincere. He's humble. He's generous. He's everything that's good about our country. So ... when I see Zach, I see the future of our country, and I think we're going to be in good hands" ("Little Red Wagon," Alchetron, https://1ref.us/kp12).

Zach Bonner
1997–

"So when they had eaten breakfast, Jesus said to Simon Peter, 'Simon, son of Jonah, do you love Me more than these?' He said to Him, 'Yes, Lord; You know that I love you.' He said to him, 'Feed My lambs.' He said to him again a second time, 'Simon, son of Jonah, do you love Me?' He said to Him, 'Yes, Lord; You know that I love You.' He said to him, 'Tend My sheep.' He said to him the third time, 'Simon, son of Jonah, do you love Me?' Peter was grieved because He said to him the third time, 'Do you love Me?' And he said to Him, 'Lord, You know all things; You know that I love You.' Jesus said to him, 'Feed My sheep'" (John 21:15–17).

22

VICTIM TO VICTOR

2009—Pendleton, Indiana

Eighth grade began the most miserable year of Brandon's life. It grew worse until every day drew him closer and closer to committing suicide. His parents knew nothing of his struggles. Mom, a fourth-grade teacher, and Dad, a police officer, would have helped had they known. All they knew was from the campaign posters Brandon made running for class president. They had been encouraged to see their shy and fearful son break out of his shell. But it was not to be.

They didn't know until later that the bullies in his middle school who had picked on him without mercy in the past, now tore up his campaign posters, wrote insulting and hateful notes on them, or dropped them in the urinals in the boys' bathroom.

Speaking of his desire to become class president, he said later, "I was a weird kid in middle school. I looked weird. I sounded weird. But pushing down feelings of self-doubt, I thought, Hey, this could be a new me." But it only made things worse.

There were "bully boxes" at school fastened to the wall in the busiest hallways. These were intended to give victims a way to report incidents without naming names. But when the bullies found out they had been reported, the problem multiplied. Brandon thought things through. If there was some way this reporting could be done in secret—like by our cell phones—it would be quicker and safer. Maybe I could build an app that kids could use. I love to work with coding. Yes! That's what I'll do. And so he did. He began working on a system by which school administrators would be notified in a private, secret way so they could be on the lookout for problems.

Meanwhile Dad and Mom found out about Brandon's concerns when he told them of his idea. Dad said, "You know, son, there's a special school at Anderson that could help you with your project. It's sponsored by our county Chamber of Commerce, and it's called the Young Entrepreneurs Academy. You could take the course along with your regular schoolwork—it wouldn't be too much for you. What do you think?"

"Well, yes, let's look into it, Dad. It sounds interesting."

So, in a few months Brandon was learning how to begin a business with his new mobile invention. They taught him organizational skills, how to schedule meetings with workers, how to meet deadlines, assigning tasks to his team, how to speak effectively, conflict resolution, creating and maintaining a shared vision, and motivating others. Not only that, but the basics of financing his own business, marketing, goalsetting and, most of all, never, never to give up. Young Entrepreneurs Academy—YEA!

As a result, Brandon, age fourteen, founded his own company called Most Beastly Studios, LLC. (LLC stands for Limited Liability Company, meaning it's owned by many members and companies, and each member shares profits, expenses, and losses.) His company now has several products, including the "Bully Box" system which a school may purchase and is made free to students. The system includes auto-generated phoning to an administrator for immediate help if facing a life-threatening situation. Also the system includes photographing capabilities. Brandon has been especially careful inventing his system so that students are completely comfortable using it.

His remote business team of five subcontractor developers have as their mission:

1. Build apps that make a difference.

2. Not games.

3. Apps that improve lives.

In advising young students who are looking to start their own business, he says:

> Never doubt yourself or your abilities. As a typical lower middle-class teenager, from central Indiana, I have built a successful business that continues to grow. We are fortunate to live in a country that still rewards hard work and ingenuity. We live in a country in which a simple idea, bundled with a refusal to give up, can produce great things. That being said, success can be measured in many different ways. For some it may be financial success. For others it may be knowledge that you made a difference in our world. Whether you are selling a belief, a service, a product, or a cause, it is imperative that you believe in yourself. In a capitalistic society, the market will provide you with significant insight. Allow your current and prospective customers/clients to direct your business. It will never work the other way around. ("Brandon Boynton," Young Entrepreneurs Academy, https://1ref.us/kp13)

Brandon Boynton
1997–

"Be ye strong therefore, and let not your hands be weak: for your work shall be rewarded" (2 Chron. 15:7).

23
NO ELECTRICITY NEEDED

2012—Saanich, British Columbia, Canada

A letter from the Philippines changed Ann's life. Her girlfriend had written, "Oh, I'm so disappointed! I've worked so hard in school, but I've not been able to study at home. It gets dark so early, and my folks can't afford electricity, so I can't study. So, I've failed my class. Now I don't know what to do."

Fifteen-year-old Ann looked up from the letter, thinking. On the shelves in front of her lay all her trinkets she'd been "playing" with since she was nine. Her dad had shown her how to handle a soldering iron safely, and she had entered local school science fairs with her inventions. Soldering transistors and figuring out how to build things had become her passion, especially making things

> *A letter from the Philippines changed Ann's life.*

that worked without house electricity. Her seventhgrade science fair project was a radio powered by wasted heat from a candle.

And now this letter from her friend! There must be some way to make light without house power, she thought. So, she looked up things in the books and found out about piezoelectricity. It says here that piezoelectricity is that which accumulates in certain solid materials under pressure. She figured, If I put two ceramic tiles together with pieces of conductor, like copper wire, in between, and if one ceramic layer is warmer than the other, the copper will produce energy. So, she built a hollow flashlight that would light up when held in a person's hand. And it worked!

Well! Suddenly, fifteen-year-old Ann's invention hit the news. A flashlight that does not need batteries! She won first place at the Google Science Fair and also at the Intel Science and Engineering Fair. She was invited to appear on *The Tonight Show* and to give three talks on TEDx. She was on *TIME* magazine's 30 Under 30 World Changers list—all before she graduated from high school! In 2016 she was voted the Popular Science Young Inventor of the Year. Later she received the Sustainable Enterprise Award.

Her next invention was the eDrink Coffee Mug that charges your cell or iPad from its heat while you wait for it to cool down. She also presented her line of children's toys that run on green energy (solar, wind, or water). Ann is the founder of Makosinski Enterprises and has patents on several of her inventions.

"Oh, I don't have any talents," you may say. But even though you think you don't have any talents, you can discover them by reviewing your interests, whether they be bugs, animals, math, literature, plants, machines, birds, music, etc. Then by experimentation, study, and hard work, you will be a success, especially if you wish to help others—like Ann helped her friend in the Philippines.

Ann Makosinski

1997–

"Then I, John, saw the holy city, New Jerusalem, coming down out of heaven from God.... I saw no temple in it, for the Lord God Almighty and the Lamb [Jesus] are its temple. The city had no

need of the sun or of the moon to shine in it, for the glory of God illuminated it. The Lamb is its light. And the nations of those who are saved shall walk in its light, and ... there shall be no night there" (Rev. 21:2, 22–25).

24
NO GIRLS ALLOWED

2008—Swat Region, Pakistan

A horrible explosion! Another girls' school blown up. The Taliban, a radical Muslim group, had already destroyed 100 girls' schools in Pakistan and had issued a public edict banning girls from going to school. Their belief system also included banning television, music, women's education, and women from going shopping. Their goal was to destroy the Pakistani government. Bodies of beheaded policemen were displayed in town squares. Something needed to be done. But what? Everyone was afraid. Many had moved away, but Ziauddin Yousafzai, an owner of a chain of private schools said, "We're not going to leave. We have to stay here and fight this thing!"

The British Broadcasting Company Urdu organized a group of workers who combined their ideas and came up with a plan that might help. They knew all the violence that was going on but didn't know much about how ordinary citizens lived under Taliban control. They decided to ask a schoolgirl to blog anonymously about her life in the Swat District. They found one girl willing to help, but when her parents found out, they forbade her to continue because it was too dangerous. Ziauddin Yousafzai, the school owner, could find no girls whose parents would allow such a thing. So, he asked his own daughter, eleven-year-old Malala, if she could do it. "Oh, yes, Father! I know lots of things that are going on in our town. I've been reading the newspapers and I've had lots of experiences myself. Yes, I'll do it. You know how I love to write."

So, she began. The BBC editors insisted she write under another name, so she chose the name "Gui Makai" which means "cornflower"; this was the name of a character in one of the country's folktales. Here is a copy of her first blog:

> I had a terrible dream yesterday with military helicopters and the Taliban. I have had such dreams since the launch of the military operation in Swat. My mother made me breakfast and I went off to school. I was afraid going to school because the Taliban had issued an edict banning all girls from attending schools. ("Moving moments from Malala's BBC diary," BBC News, https://1ref.us/kp14)

Only eleven out of twenty-seven girls attended class because of the Taliban's edict. Malala's three friends shifted to Peshawar, Lahore, and Rawalpindi with their families because of the Taliban's edict.

The following day, she read for the first time, excerpts from her blog published in a local newspaper. Several more schools were destroyed. Fewer girls showed up at Malala's school, and it shut down. She was soon asked to give interviews on television and in the newspapers. She became known as an effective education activist, as young as she was. She was nominated for the International Children's Peace Prize by activist Desmond Tutu. A *New York Times* documentary about her life appeared when the Pakistan Armed Forces (Army, Navy, Airforce) launched an attack on the Taliban to protect Malala's home, Swat District.

In October 2012, while Malala and two girlfriends rode a bus home from taking an exam, a gunman approached and demanded, "Which of you is Malala?" Then he shot all three girls. He shot Malala in the head. Malala was rushed to the hospital. The other girls were not as seriously hurt. Malala remained unconscious and in critical condition for many days. She was moved to Birmingham, U.K. (United Kingdom or England) where the doctors did several surgeries on her. She finally regained consciousness and recovered.

International anger and concern were aroused against the Taliban. The gunman was never found. A group of Muslim clerics reproached the assassination attempt, but the Taliban replied that they would do it again, because they said it was a "religious obligation." This fueled even more outrage and condemnation toward them.

Malala received the 2012 Sakharov Prize for Freedom of Thought, named after the Russian scientist. In 2014 she was awarded the Nobel Peace Prize, the youngest person (at age seventeen) to be so honored. *TIME* magazine included her for three years in their list of the "100 Most Influential People."

She stayed in England and finished high school, then went on to Oxford University, graduating in 2020 with a major in Philosophy, Politics, and Economics. Malala has continued her goal of helping to educate children. In 2019 an estimated 260 million children around the world don't have a chance to get an education; most of it is caused by social inequality. While in Birmingham, she and her dad created the Malala Fund. It supports the education of thousands of children around the world.

Malala says she has forgiven the Taliban for their treatment of her and of so many innocent people. She said, "I hope that their own children will be able to get a good education." She was almost murdered but came up wavin' the flag! Could you do the same?

Malala Yousafzai
1997–

> *"You have heard that it was said, 'You shall love your neighbor and hate your enemy.' But I say to you, love your enemies, bless those who curse you, do good to those who hate you, and pray for those who spitefully use you and persecute you, that you may be sons of your Father in heaven; for He makes His sun rise on the evil and on the good, and sends rain on the just and on the unjust.... Therefore you shall be perfect, just as your Father in heaven is perfect"* (Matt. 5:43–45, 48).

25

WARM HOMES IN WINTER

2008—Westerly, Rhode Island

Money was difficult to earn up north. No matter how hard people worked, it still was not enough to keep the family healthy and comfortable. The charities were running out of funds so they could do little to help.

School was warm enough, though, if the students wore more than one layer of clothing. Cassandra, ten years old, listened to her fifth-grade teacher talking about how to keep warm at home. Oil burners were used by most families, but oil was hard to get for a decent price. "What we need is to recycle the used cooking oil that every family throws away," she said.

Cassandra looked around at a few of her closest friends, shook her head yes, and whispered, "Let's do it!" So, after school they got together and began to plan how they could begin to collect used cooking oil.

"I can bring what my mom has," said Cassandra.

"Yeah, my mom made doughnuts yesterday. There's quite a bit at our house," one of the boys said.

"Why couldn't we go to McDonald's? They're always frying stuff!" exclaimed another.

"We could pour it all in a big plastic container and have it carted off to be cleaned and recycled," a girl said. "My folks have a big plastic garbage can that we could wash up and use." Sure enough, Cassandra's team soon had enough to truck off to a company that recycled used cooking oil.

One evening at home, she told her folks of the progress she and her friends had made, Dad said, "Maybe you could start a nonprofit company."

But he couldn't finish because Cassandra had jumped up out of her chair, her face shining, "Yes! We could call it Turn Grease Into Fuel—TGIF!"

"You got it, kid!" Dad exclaimed.

So, the small group of her school friends expanded their work, and a nearby company chemically refined all the used cooking oil into safe fuel. Then charity organizations were able to distribute the heating oil to needy families.

Soon the project had grown so fast that the TGIF kids went to the Rhode Island legislature with a bill that made conserving used cooking oil and turning it into heating fuel a law! In January 2012 the new law came into effect. Reducing waste and helping more than 500 families brought TGIF and Cassandra to the attention of the entire nation. Recycling centers have sprung up everywhere. In fact, 500,000 gallons of biodiesel are now fueling farm equipment, machinery, trucks, and tractors!

Cassandra has received many environmental awards, including appearances on CNN, TEDxEast, and even a "Women of Worth" award from the Loreal Company. She said, "Being a Woman of Worth means joining an incredible group of empowering women and working even harder to provide homes in my community with basic necessities" ("Cassandra Lin," L'Oréal Paris, https://www.lorealparisusa.com/women-of-worth/honorees/2017/cassandra-lin).

Cassandra Lin

1998–

"Even a child is known by his doings, whether his work be pure, and whether it be right" (Prov. 20:11, KJV).

26

GOTTA HAVE SOLE

2003—Cranston, Rhode Island

Mother cleared the breakfast table after Dad had left for work. Her five-year-old son played with his cars on the floor. "Nicholas, how would you like to go with me to visit some families in town that don't have any home?"

"Don't have any home?" asked the boy, who could not imagine anyone with no home.

"Yes, there are people that don't have any money to rent or buy a place to live."

"Don't have any money?" He looked up at his mother. "They don't have a job like Dad?"

"Well, some of them don't have a dad. There are many reasons why some people have no money—sickness, lost family members, divorce—some have come from other countries far away and don't know our language well enough to get a job. Oh, there are lots of reasons. Our city has a special place where they can live until their life gets better and they can move into a home of their own. Anyway, let's go see if there's anything we can do to help them."

"Okay. Can I wear my new shoes that light up when I walk?"

"Oh, I think you'd better wear your old shoes. Some of those children may not have any shoes at all, and you would make them sad."

So, off they went to the homeless shelter in town. Mother helped the ladies working there with cooking and cleaning. Nicholas stayed near his mother because he was rather scared. The people wore raggedy clothes and shoes. Some had no shoes at all, especially the children. When Mother's work was done, they went home. They both took showers, washed their hair, and put on clean clothes. Mother threw the clothes they had worn into the washing machine. "What can we do to help those children, Nicholas?" she asked as she began preparing the evening meal.

"The kids don't have good shoes. Some don't have any shoes at all," he replied. "I'd like to give them my shoes."

"And some of your clothes?"

"Yes!"

> *"Oh! I know exactly what I want to do!" he exclaimed, "I'm going to get shoes for homeless children!"*

And that's what he did. He helped clean out his closet. But he kept thinking about all those kids with no shoes. When he got older, the problem still rankled his conscience.

When he turned thirteen, he looked forward to his Bar Mitzvah, the Jewish celebration for boys growing into adulthood. His rabbi instructed him saying, "Now it's time for you to take on grown-up responsibilities. Along with your duties as an adult, you need to choose some kind of service project to help other people."

"Oh! I know exactly what I want to do!" he exclaimed, "I'm going to get shoes for homeless children!" And that's what he did. He went to the local shoe store and asked, "Do you have any shoes you could give for the kids in the homeless shelter?"

"We sure do, young man. You just wait here, and we'll get you some!"

He went to all the stores, wrote to shoe companies, and soon had enough. That's when he started the charity called Gotta Have Sole providing new shoes for homeless kids.

One of the first to get a new pair was Matt who went to school every other day and his sister went the other days. They had only one pair between them—a girls' pair with pink sparklies. Matt would get so embarrassed when the guys would dance around him like ballet dancers. But when Nicholas gave him a new pair of basketball shoes, everything changed. Matt was able to catch up on his schoolwork and now hopes to go to college.

Nicholas works out of his family's garage filling orders. The boxes of shoes are organized according to size and whether they are for boys or girls. The last report from Gotta Have Sole is that more than 99,000 pairs of new shoes have been sent to homeless kids all over the USA. Several youth groups have joined Nicholas in his efforts.

He has received many awards, a couple of which have been college scholarships, including World of Children Award, PBTEEN Extraordinary Teens, Nickelodeon Halo Award, Caring Award, Charlotte Bacon Art of Caring Award, Peace First Prize and Fellowship, Muhammad Ali Humanitarian Award, CNN Hero Young Wonder, Diller Teen Tikkun Olam Award, Myra Kraft Community MFV Award, USA Today National Make a Difference Honoree, President's Volunteer Service Award-Gold Level, and many others.

The little boy who couldn't wear his light-up shoes to the homeless shelter has seen many homeless children hug the new shoes he has given them.

Nicholas Lowinger
1998–

"He who has pity on the poor lends to the LORD; and He will pay back what he has given" (Prov. 19:17).

27

THE SUPERKIDPRENEUR

2004—Atlanta, Georgia

As Dad placed his new computer on his desk, the old computer lay on the floor looking neglected and rejected. Maya asked, "What are you going to do with this old one, Daddy?"

"Well, I haven't decided yet. Do you have any ideas?"

"Can I take it apart?"

Dad looked up suddenly. Why does my four-year-old want to take apart a computer instead of playing with her dolls? He asked, "Why do you want to do that?"

"I want to see what's inside. It knows so many things." She turned it over and put her finger on one of the screws.

"Well, that would be fun. Shall we do it together?" Being a computer technician, Dad knew the dangers, especially if she plugged it in. So, they took it apart, Dad explaining the pieces, Maya asking questions as a "pre-geek" would.

> *Dad looked up suddenly. Why does my four-year-old want to take apart a computer instead of playing with her dolls? He asked, "Why do you want to do that?"*

"In fact, Maya," he added, "You love to draw. You could make your flipbooks a lot easier because this new machine will help you draw your pictures faster." From then on, her excitement knew no bounds!

As she grew older, Mother taught her how to sew. Now she kept an eye out for pieces of ribbon, unused fabric, and materials to make scarves and hats. She put them on and wore them away from home, and ladies stopped and asked, "Say! Where did you get that cute hat?"

She would say, "My mother taught me to sew, and I made it myself."

One lady said, "Well, I'd love to have a hat like that! Could you make me one? I would pay you for it."

Maya ran home, bursting through the front door. "Mom! Dad! That lady wants me to make her a hat like mine, and she said she would pay me! Can I do it?"

"You certainly can," her parents replied.

"Can I make a whole bunch of hats and scarves and sell them?"

"Yes, you could go into business!" added Dad, not knowing the life-changing idea he had just given to his daughter. From there, eight-year-old Maya organized a company. Dad helped her learn advertising on the computer, and Mom helped her set up a sewing room and office on the back porch.

But that isn't all. She kept thinking about the flipbooks she had loved to make when she was younger. "Dad," she asked one day, "Could you teach me how to draw pictures with the computer?"

"Sure! What are you thinking?"

"Well, I'd love to make flipbooks. I could sell them too."

"Okay, girl, go for it!" So, she added that to her business which she called "Maya's Ideas." She became a professional animator. She featured on her website a "book" called *The Pollinators* with bees as the heroes. Then she made another "book" with viruses as the enemies (which had attacked her own computer so she had to get a new one). This was even more popular and was called *Malicious Dishes*.

Her enthusiasm for protecting the environment has made her famous—using leftover materials for her creations and encouraging others to avoid wasting available resources in all they do and by giving speeches. She has even used her digital animated programs to encourage people to save the natural beauties of the earth. She was the first person to present a digital report to Congress encouraging them to build a Women's History Museum in Washington.

Her awards and appearances are too numerous to list here, but they include CNN, CBS, NPR, Forbes, *TIME*, Disney Channel, TED talks, etc. She has probably made more money than anyone her age, but she donates a large portion of it to help people and to protect the environment.

She says, "You always, always, always have to start with a passion because if you don't have a passion, a love or drive behind what you're doing, then eventually it's going to go downhill, and you won't want to do it anymore. It's really important to do what you love because you'll go farther" (Becky Chung, "This 13-year-old entrepreneur is out to change the world: A Q&A with Maya Penn," TED Conferences, https://1ref.us/kp16).

She also says:

> Everyone can make a change. It doesn't matter who you are, where you came from, how old you are—every single person can make a change if they have a passion for it. People in general, youths especially, are really oblivious to the problems that are happening around the world. Even if they are [aware], they might not know what they can do to make a change. So really investigate and get more informed. (Ibid.)

Maya Penn
2000–

"For it is God who works in you both to will and to do for His good pleasure" (Phil. 2:13).

28

NETTING THE GOAL

2012—Boca Raton, Florida

"Oh, no!" cried twelve-year-old Rachel. The hard lacrosse ball she had pitched into her net training rebounder had broken right through the net into Mother's flower garden. "That's the second time that's happened! It's like I'm getting punished for doing it right!" She looked over the damage, thinking, I know I can't ask Mom and Dad for another one. This one cost them $300. What am I going to do? I love playing lacrosse, but I've got to practice. The coaches say to bounce the ball against the house, but I could break windows. Maybe I could make one—only stronger. I could double the strings on the net. It would hold better. Yes! That's what I'll do. Make my own! As she started for the house, she stopped suddenly. Hey! I wonder how many other people have broken their rebounder! I could … could … Yes! Yes! I could make a whole bunch and sell them! They told us at school to work on an idea and if it's something you really love … if it's honest and helpful … Yes! I'll do it!

And she did.

Lacrosse is the fastest growing sport in the United States. It's similar to field hockey except the stick has a basket on the end that can scoop up the ball from the ground by the front end and on the other end of the basket there's a bag that holds the ball until it's shot out. The team goal is to keep the ball away from the opposing team and to propel it past the goalie into the net.

Mother was a successful lawyer, and Dad ran his own business called TouchSuite, a Point of Sale (POS) company that sold systems that helped list customers' purchases on a machine at the store, took credit card or cash, and gave them a receipt. It helped the store owners keep accurate records and notified them if the supply on the shelves was getting too low. Hotels used them in rooms so occupants could order service, food, or pay their bill.

Restaurants might have a machine at their tables on which diners could order meals.

Then Rachel attended a thirty-three-week course for middle and high school students called Young Entrepreneurs' Academy (YEA!) that they could take while doing their regular schoolwork. The students learned how to generate ideas, plan, do market research, and found their own companies. There are nineteen cities in the United States that offer YEA! (at this writing), and it has produced many successful young businesspeople.

So, Rachel went ahead and built her first lacrosse goal net and a rebounder using stronger netting and poles. She also built more to sell. She built them herself at a factory to save money for herself and her customers. She did not do advertising except by word-of-mouth and by her friends on social media who spread the word for her. She called her new company Gladiator Lacrosse. How old was she? Thirteen years old!

Then a new idea struck. "Hey, Dad! Why don't I go to the games with a bunch of these and sell them on the spot?"

"You can do it!" replied Dad, "We'll set up the family tent and you can go for it!"

"But ... but, I'd have to borrow some money from you."

"I think you have a good, practical idea, and, yes, I'll lend you enough to get started."

Her first sale at a game turned out well. She said, "Kids who lose games want to practice more. You're walking off the field, and you see two pieces of equipment you need to take your game to the next level. So that was a no-brainer for us." In fact, her idea paid off at her first lacrosse tournament weekend when she made $10,000 in sales!

Within a year Rachel had paid off her debt to her father and her company was worth $200,000. At the end of the second year, it was worth a million dollars!

She received her first public relations story from the *South Florida Business Journal*, and from there she appeared in *Entrepreneur* magazine, then *TIME* magazine, followed by *New York Times*, and *USA Today*. Then she was approached by ABC's *Shark Tank*, and she appeared on Season 7, Episode 28. And from there, more and more success until today, she is worth more than 5 million dollars! And she's been going to high school and college in the meantime!

The little twelve-year-old soccer player practicing in her back yard had no idea what her future would hold when the ball broke through the net!

Rachel Zietz
2000–

"And you shall remember the LORD your God, for it is He who gives you power to get wealth, that He may establish His covenant which He swore to your fathers, as it is this day" (Deut. 8:18).

29

FIT TO BE TIED

2010—Memphis, Tennessee

The sun-drenched mall grew more crowded as the afternoon progressed. Mother and nine-year-old Mo stepped into a men's store. Dad was a classy dresser and Mo had inherited his taste for a snappy appearance. Today, Mo and Mom were looking for a bowtie for Mo to wear to his sixth-grade graduation into middle school.

Mom shook her head. "I'm sorry, son. All the ties we've seen today are all just too expensive. We can't afford to spend what little money we have on these kinds of purchases."

Mo looked down. Mother was right. "But … but …" He stopped and looked up, his face shining. "Hey! Maybe Gramma would make me one!"

"That's an idea. We have fabric at home, and you could pick out just what you want."

"Yeah! Let's go!"

Grandma, who had been a seamstress for years, said, "Sure. I'll help you. But you know what? I'm sure you can make your own. I'll teach you how. You can use my sewing machine." Mo didn't know, nor did Mother and Grandma know, that that moment would change their lives!

At the party, his classmates said to him, "Hey, Mo, where'd you get that snazzy tie?"

"I made it."

"You made it? Wow! I like it!"

When he got home, crashing through the front door, he shouted, "Hey, Mom! Gramma! The kids liked my tie! Some of them said they'd like me to make them one! I could even sell them to people! Gramma, can I use your sewing machine some more?"

"You sure can. And you can use all the fabric you want. In fact, if you want to sell a lot of them, I'll lend you the money to buy more."

Mother added, "I'm sure the stores in town will sell them for you."

So, that's how Mo's Bows came to be. Soon he had made enough profit to pay Grandma back and to buy his own sewing machine. He began to go to the stores and buy his own fabric, not just plain material, but all kinds of interesting prints, a policy he has followed ever since. His business grew to the point where he had to hire people to sew for him, including Grandma. Mother took orders while he was in school. Then he came home and worked at his business—sewing, planning, writing ads, buying material. By the time he was eleven years old, he had sold 2,000 bowties.

> *By the time he was eleven years old, he had sold 2,000 bowties.*

That was when things started exploding. He was invited to appear on NBC's *Shark Tank* by Daymond John. Mother was with him. The interview went so well that Mo's Bows took flight. Daymond John offered to teach him how to do more advertising, how to manage his business, and how to improve his business sense. Daymond also encouraged him to advertise on eBay, ETSY, and Amazon.

Mo loves basketball. (In fact, by the time he was twenty, he was almost seven feet tall!) One year, for the National Basketball Association's Draft, several of the players wore Mo's Bows, which eventually led to his signing a contract with NBA for his ties that ran into the seven digits. The quality of his ties is so good that customers keep coming back.

He has since appeared on *The Steve Harvey Show*, *Good Morning America*, CBS *This Morning*, the Disney Channel, and has been featured in *Business Week*, *Black Enterprise Inc.*, and *O, The Oprah Magazine*. He was included in *TIME's* "30 Most Influential Teens," and *Fortune's* "18 Under 18." He was inducted into the Tennessee State Museum's Costume and Textiles Institute. And most interesting of all, President Obama invited him to the inaugural White House Dems Day, where Mo gave the president a blue bowtie called "Obama Blue."

Now Mo has started Go Mo! It's a scholarship fund to send children from Memphis to summer camp. Can you believe the nine-year-old who couldn't afford a tie for a party is now a multimillionaire?

Moziah Bridges
2001–

"As for every man to whom God has given riches and wealth, and given him power to eat of it, to receive his heritage and rejoice in his labor—this is the gift of God" (Eccles. 5:19).

30

SMART KID, SMART MACHINE

2016—India

Traveling to India with his parents was, for Neil, a great privilege just before entering high school. Visiting relatives in that country revealed to him the great needs of the people, especially the farmers, as they toiled all day in the blistering sun. "But we have to do it to provide for our families," explained his grandpa.

Neil knew that he himself could not survive even one day working at that backbreaking, skin-burning field work. "Look at Uncle's back and arms!" he exclaimed. Right then and there thirteen-year-old Neil received his life calling from his wise Creator in heaven.

When he arrived home, he entered high school at Moravian Academy in Bethlehem, Pennsylvania, where students of all beliefs were educated—Muslim, Jewish, Christian—and some who didn't know what they believed.

As he answered questions during his entrance interview, he said, "I've been to a country where there are not only crop diseases, but people with skin diseases, and I want to help people get rid of all that, especially people around the world who are too poor to know how to get help."

"How do you plan to do that?" asked the interviewer.

"Well, along with the other studies I must learn here, I want to work on a way to observe plant diseases from handheld phones and a way to answer the farmer regarding what to do about his sick plants."

"Well, that sounds complicated, especially for one as young as you."

"Oh, I've learned a lot about computers at Moravian grade school. Now I'm investigating artificial intelligence where computers can solve problems."

From then on, through his years in high school and during summer vacations, Neil worked with teams, teachers, and mentors. Here, in his own fourteen-year-old super language, is what happened: "Technical Lead. Open Agriculture (OpenAg) Initiative September 2016 to May 2017—nine months. Moravian Academy, Bethlehem, PA. OpenAg has a mission to create healthier, more engaging, more inventive future food systems. It believes the precursor to a healthier and more sustainable food system will be the creation of an opensource ecosystem of food technologies that enable and promote transparency, networked experimentation, education, and hyper-local production. Working with a team of nerd farmers we built the nation's first high school food computer (which we affectionately call 'Foam Computer') at Moravian Academy. I was involved in configuring the hardware and programming various sensors and actuators."

Later he wrote, "LaunchX: High School Entrepreneur Programs. Student Champion. September 2016 to September 2019—three years and one month. Moravian Academy. I am currently in charge of guiding companies at my school entrepreneurship club. I teach jumpstart student companies as well as provide leadership and advice for students looking to apply for entrepreneurial ventures and endeavors in the area."

From 2017–2022, Neil founded his company to help the world's farmers. Here is his advertisement: "PlantumAI is an app that is able to detect, diagnose, and provide treatment options for plant diseases straight from your phone. If you're a farmer who needs help figuring what strain of disease, or what nutritional deficiency, is destroying your harvest, PlantumAI will be able to provide agricultural advice" ("PLANTUMAI," Neil Deshmukh, https://1ref.us/kp17).

Also, in June of 2017, Neil began research on how to help low-vision sufferers, including some members of his own family. He worked with others until 2020 at Massachusetts Institute of Technology where he attended college. He co-founded VocalEyes to help people who are partially blind navigate their surroundings and read.

Then he invented a low-cost device ($150) called BAYMAX that can identify diseases in humans such as heart, skin, and brain diseases (1,500 in all), including what to do in emergency situations. This helps doctors save time, money, and lives, especially in the less fortunate areas of the world.

Neil has received so many Grand Awards and honors, including the United States Presidential Scholar—too many to include here. He says, "I am dedicated to identifying societal problems that have remained overlooked, and developing comprehensive solutions that incorporate novel technologies and community involvement, to help people around our world" ("ABOUT ME," Neil Deshmukh, https://www.neildeshmukh.com/about).

Neil Deshmukh
2003–

"I put on righteousness, and it clothed me; my justice was like a robe and a turban. I was eyes to the blind, and I was feet to the lame. I was a father to the poor, and I searched out the case that I did not know" (Job 29:14–16).

31

LITTLE GIRL INVENTOR

2015—Lone Tree, Colorado

Watching the news on television with her parents was an enjoyable break for Gitanjali, of Eastern Indian descent. Being busy with school, Girl Scouts, 4-H Club, playing piano for residents of the local assisted living center, cooking, and classical Indian dancing should be enough for a ten-year-old, but when she heard about the serious water situation in Flint, Michigan, she sat up and exclaimed, "All those people getting so sick! And all the little kids! What are they going to do to help them?"

Dad and Mother, both expert information technologists, looked at their daughter. "Well," replied Dad, "they are going to have to find a way to help the people test the lead content in the water coming out of their faucets. Oh, there are tapes that can be immersed in the water, but then when they send them into the lab, it might take weeks to get an answer."

Mother added, "Yes, it's a dangerous situation. It can affect little children so much that it causes brain damage."

"It even causes Alzheimer's in older folks," added Dad. "As they said on TV, Flint has always obtained their water from the Detroit water system, but because Flint was having financial problems, they've gone back to their own antiquated system with old lead pipes that are deteriorating."

"Then they need a way to tell if there's lead in their water without waiting for weeks while everybody in the family is getting sick."

Gitanjani looked down at her hands, then looked up. "We've been learning in science class about nanotubes."

"And what are you learning?"

"Well, they are microscopic particles made of carbon. They are super strong and can react to chemicals. Do you think there might be a chance that they could find lead?"

"What are you thinking, Gitanjali?"

"If there was a device that could find lead coming out of a faucet...."

"Honey! You got it! You can put one together. I know you can! We'll help when you need it, but you can do it!" exclaimed both parents, jumping to their feet.

So, she did! She gathered all the information she could get from her computer. She found she needed a nine-volt battery, a lead sensing unit using carbon nanotubes, a Bluetooth extension, and a processor. She put it all together and took it to her computer science teacher. He said later, "In the beginning, she just brought in all these wires and set them down on the table. I looked at it and said, 'You need a case.' So, I connected her to the engineering teacher where she learned how to make one with a 3-D printer." Now her little machine (called a Tethys after the Greek goddess of clean water) is housed in a blue 3-D printed plastic box. Her computer teacher worked with her after school to develop a user-friendly app to communicate the degree of lead contamination which connects to a smartphone. And the whole thing worked!

She has been honored with many awards, including "America's Top Young Scientist" 2016, was featured on the *Tonight Show* where she demonstrated her Tethys invention 2017, won the Discovery Education 3M Young Scientist Challenge ($25,000) (for Middle School students) 2017, was recognized as one of the recipients of Forbes 30 Under 30 2018. She presented her idea at the MAKERS Conference 2018. She received the President's Environmental Youth Award of US Environmental Protection Agency 2019, the Top "Health" Pillar Prize for the TCS Ignite Innovation Student Challenge (For her work in early diagnosis of prescription opioid addiction) 2020. She was *TIME's* first ever Kid of the Year with her picture on the cover 2020, and Laureate of the Young Activists Summit at United Nations Geneva. She is a three-time TEDx (Technology, Entertainment and Design) speaker.

She attends the STEM School (Science, Technology, Engineering and Mathematics) in Highlands Ranch, Colorado. with 1,800 K-12 students from Denver. She is doing research at the University of Colorado and wants to study genetics and epidemiology at Massachusetts Institute of Technology.

She is working on an artificial intelligence project called Kindly to detect potential cyberbullying. Also, she's working to earn her pilot's license.

> *From contamination of water to cyberbullying and education equality, I believe that each one of us can take small steps to address the problems with whatever talents we have.*

She is quoted as saying, "From contamination of water to cyberbullying and education equality, I believe that each one of us can take small steps to address the problems with whatever talents we have" (Gitanjali Rao, "Gitanjali Rao, the young scientist using innovation to advocate for children's rights," Voices of Youth, https://1ref.us/kp19); "Observe, brainstorm, research, build, and communicate" (TIME staff, "Meet TIME's First-Ever Kid of the Year," TIME USA, https://1ref.us/kp20).

Gitanjali Rao
2005–

> *"I will instruct you and teach you in the way you should go; I will guide you with My eye"* (Ps. 32:8).

32

WARM BATH

2014—San Cristóbal de las Chiapas, Southern Mexico

A special school excited four-year-old Xochitl (pronounced soh-chee, and I'm going to write like it sounds). She loved science especially because she wanted to be a scientist. Mom and Dad had helped by sending her to a special class called Adopt a Talent Program (PAUTA). The teachers and mentors worked zealously to help their students develop their ideas, make plans, and organize their strategy. Sohchee loved every minute of that class! Her first project at four years old was to organize a special place at home for a lab. She was given an extra room which she furnished with just the right equipment.

"I know what I want to work on first," she told her mother. "I want to see if I can make some sweet-smelling stuff from our flowers. They smell so good, and maybe I can cook them and put it in a jar … I don't know if that will work, but if it doesn't, I'll try some other way."

Mom replied, "Go for it, honey. I'll help if you need it. Just be careful."

She went out and began collecting flowers. Experiments began and finally she came up with a beautiful-smelling mixture she called "Xochitl's Essence." And what do you know! She won first prize at the PAUTA State Fair! She was so excited that she trembled when the founder of PAUTA came to shake her hand and congratulate her.

One evening, a few years later when Sohchee was in third grade, Dad had come home from his teaching job and was reading the newspaper. Sohchee came in and sat at his feet. "Dad, I'm working on another idea."

Dad put down his paper and leaned over. "What's going on in that brain of yours now, sweetie?"

"Well, we've been talking in school about how poor everybody is here."

"That's right, our state of Chiapas is the poorest region in all of the thirty-two regions in Mexico. They say it's because there are so few people from other regions and countries moving in to give new ideas, principles, and standards to our people."

"Some of the kids in my class are so skinny … and dirty. Their folks have to cut down trees for firewood to keep warm and to cook, but they can't get enough to take warm baths."

"Yes," said Dad as he leaned back in his chair. "That's the way it is here. It's been said that only about 30 percent of Mexican young people graduate from high school. They have to go out and hunt for jobs."

"And there's a lot of sickness. Some families don't have water, and even if they did and tried to take a bath or shower, the water is so cold … and they get sick. Anyway, Dad, we do have sunshine."

"What are you thinking, kid?"

"Well, is there any way the sun could heat water?"

And that was the beginning of Sohchee's greatest invention—warming water with sunshine!

At her next Adopt a Talent class, she presented her idea and was told to map out a plan in her notebook, make a list of things she needed and where to get them. She gathered plastic water bottles, a black hose, plastic cable ties, wood for a base, glass doors from an old cooler, and an old black nylon sheet—all from the garbage dump!

"But, Dad, I don't have any black paint. I need to paint the bottles."

"I'll get you some." Dad was getting excited. "Do you want me to help you put it up on the roof of our house when you get it built?"

"Oh, yes!"

So, she put it all together. They moved it up to the roof. The hot sun did its part, and soon there was warm water! It worked! She called her invention "Warm Bath." Mom and Dad invited the neighbors, and soon they were all making their own water heaters! About thirty dollars was all it took to get warm water for each family. What a celebration!

As a result, the suffering poor can keep healthy without having to cut trees and build fires. The high rate of lung illnesses has been reduced, and the climate change has slowed down with trees preserved.

And you know what? In 2018 Sohchee won two first prizes—PAUTA again, and she was the first child to receive a most important prize from the National Autonomous University of Mexico (UNAM) Institute of Nuclear Science that awards Mexican women of science who accomplish extraordinary work and research!

Do you think the God of heaven smiled on this eight-year-old for working to improve the lives of the poorest of the poor? Absolutely!

Xochitl Guadalupe Cruz Lopez
2010–

"And the King shall answer ... them, Verily I say unto you, Inasmuch as ye have done it unto one of the least of these ... ye have done it unto Me" (Matt. 25:40, KJV).

33

THE BEAST

2020—Chad, Central Africa

"Yay!" shouted the four children when Dad asked, "How would you like to go back to the United States and visit your grandparents?"

"When can we go?" they asked, jumping up and down, and hugging Dad and Mom.

"Well, as soon as we can get ready," replied Mom. "We'll be gone most of the year, so we'll have to keep on doing some schoolwork."

"Oh, that's okay," said eleven-year-old Lyol. Eight-year-old Zane, seven-year-old Addison, and four-year-old Juniper all agreed.

Both parents were missionary physicians. Olen, an emergency room specialist, and his wife, Danae, a maternity doctor, served in Chad, one of the poorest countries in the world, politically unstable and violent. The people struggled against ignorance and poverty. Missionaries worked under constant stress, dealing with people's diseases, health issues, accidents, crime, and death. After ten years of such experiences, a sabbatical was desperately needed for the Netteburgs.

As they were packing to leave, Olen turned to his wife and exclaimed, "Hey! I've got an idea! Let's see if the kids would want to hike the Adirondack Trail!"

"Oh, that would be fun! But it's a long way to do the whole thing. From Maine to Georgia might be a bit much. They may not want to go that far or be able to. But, yes, let's ask them."

Well, that brought on more YAYS! and jumping. "Let's go!" they shouted.

"Okay, let's try it, if you are willing to eat just basic camp food—no milkshakes or potatoes and gravy," said Mother.

"And sleeping in sleeping bags on hard ground when it's cold, and having to carry heavy backpacks," added Dad.

"Yes! Yes!" was the response.

Dad then said, "It will take several months, and the going can be pretty rough. So, we'll see how you're doing after the first month. If it's too much, then we'll decide what to do."

Mother asked, "What about you, Juniper?"

"I want to do it! You won't have to carry me. I can do it!" the four-year-old said with great confidence. Standing forty-three inches tall and weighing forty-four pounds, she didn't know the high mountains she had to climb, some 4,000 feet up, or the slippery rocks she had to walk on crossing streams or the bears, snakes, or wild pigs she might encounter.

"Okay," replied Dad. "We'll take some practice runs while we're at Grandma and Grandpa's place in Pennsylvania, and learn what we need to take, how to pack and carry our supplies, how to cook, and clean up our campsites and ourselves."

"Oh, we can learn trees and birds and things for our Pathfinder honors too!" chimed in eight-year-old Zane, having learned about the Boy-Scout-type club back in the States.

> *Standing forty-three inches tall and weighing forty-four pounds, she didn't know the high mountains she had to climb, some 4,000 feet up, or the slippery rocks she had to walk on crossing streams or the bears, snakes, or wild pigs she might encounter.*

So it was. The family arrived in Pennsylvania in February 2020, and began taking day hikes in spite of winter weather and practiced getting organized. Then they went down to Virginia to begin. They didn't hike from south to north in one straight line, but section by section. If one section had been closed because of COVID, they would go to another section and come back later when it had reopened.

They didn't see all the natural habitat that is named there, and they did not encounter any danger from wild things. The larger animals in the Adirondack Park and along the trail are bear, deer, elk, and moose. Some of the smaller animals are beavers, squirrels, otters, chipmunks, porcupines, bobcats, foxes, woodchucks, and raccoons.

Birds along the trail include wild turkeys, ruffed grouse, mourning doves, ravens, eagles, owls, hawks, wood ducks, and warblers. Trees along the way, as the animals, depending on the climate and elevation, include oak, poplar, maple, birch, cedar, spruce, and fir.

What experiences! Never to be forgotten! "Yes, it was an amazing family adventure," said Olen Netteburg. "Our goal was to keep the kids happy and fed and warm and well-slept and dry. We did a pretty good job at that, at least at the beginning. Their legs would get tired and so we'd stop early and then have fun setting up the campsite.... But the more we got into it and the stronger our legs became, the better they all got at hiking longer distances" (Brian Metzler, "How a 4-year-old hiked the length of the Appalachian Trail," Advnture, https://1ref.us/kp21).

One day, four-year-old Juniper sat down at the foot of a mountain and started to cry. "Juniper! What's wrong? Are you getting too tired?" They all gathered around her. She didn't answer. "Don't you feel good, honey?" No answer. The tears kept coming.

Finally, after some time, she looked up and said, "Mommy is carrying my backpack, but I want to carry it myself."

"Oh, I'm sorry, Honey. I thought it would save you from getting too tired," said Mother. "Here, you take it if you want to. I'm sorry." Happily, Juniper took it, put it on her back, then beat the rest of the family to the top!

It took them a total of seventy-seven days to complete the trip. Some days they would go just a few miles, other days more. When the way was especially difficult some days and everybody seemed tired, Mom and Dad would let the kids sleep in the next morning as long as they wanted. Fourteen different days, they hiked twenty miles. After befriending another thru-hiker named Cascade on August 31, they got excited about doing thirty miles. "It wasn't an easy day," said Dad. "It was mostly flat, but it was rockier than we expected it to be, so it took us a lot longer than we thought. It took us about seventeen hours to complete it, but we enjoyed it."

Thru-hikers on the Appalachian Trail traditionally receive trail names. Addison became "Angel Wings," Zane was "Boomerang," Lyol took on "Blaze," and Juniper became "The Beast." Eventually Mom became "Queen Bee," and Dad was "Lion King."

"Being out on the trail for that long gave me a sense of peace," Danae said. "Living in Chad, we deal with a lot of situations that you don't see in the US. We deal with a lot of illnesses and deaths that could be preventable, and that's a hard thing as a doctor and as a human being, so I think you carry that weight. So, for me, being on the trail with our family, I was able to find a bit of peace and slow down and enjoy being in nature." (Ibid.)

When it was done, they had hiked the entire 2,193-mile length of the Adirondack Trail, loving every minute of it! And four-year-old Juniper? She did it all on her own two little feet!

Juniper Netteburg

2016–

> "*Prepare the way of the LORD; make straight in the desert a highway for our God. Every valley shall be exalted and every mountain and hill brought low; the crooked places shall be made straight and the rough places smooth*" (Isa. 40:3–4).

34

LITTLE MAN

2018—Lynchburg, Virginia

It was an adventure for two-year-old Harvey to take his dad's hand and go for a walk along a country road in the warmth of the Virginia sunshine. His little legs kept going as fast as he could make them go, because there was so much to see!

Dad went slowly so Harvey could keep up and stopped so they could rest or talk about a wildflower blooming by the road or a butterfly they had seen. Mother Cassie came too. "Look here, Harvey! Look how this vine is climbing right up the trunk of this tree." And Harvey would reach out and touch the leaves.

Josh, Harvey's dad, said to Mother one day, "It's amazing how this boy is growing. His little legs are getting longer and stronger every day. I bet he could attack even the Adirondack Trail and get there before we could get started!" They both laughed. But the joke eventually turned into a dream.

"Do you really think he could do it?" they asked each other. "Maybe in another year or two," they concluded. So, the joke became a goal.

Josh and Cassie began saving every dollar they could to put in the bank so they could take time off from their real estate business to hike the Adirondack Trail from Georgia to Maine—2,193 miles!

"This is crazy!" Cassie exclaimed.

Josh replied, "Yeah, but we're crazy people. Let's see how Harvey grows. We'll get him used to walking here at home and...."

Cassie added, "And we'll feed him right, set up a routine...."

"And get us all used to camping," Josh said. "Okay! Let's do it!"

And they did. By January of Harvey's fourth year, the family started the trail at its beginning in Springer Mountain, Georgia. They decided to walk ten miles a day, stopping at campsites that are placed by the Adirondack Trail organization. Some of the sites have three-sided shelters with wooden floors for hikers to sleep in. Harvey had gone to a Dollar General store and bought himself a calculator so he could keep track of the miles.

> *One of the hikers organized a treasure hunt for Harvey, hiding toys and glow sticks, drawing maps for him along the way.*

Harvey had the time of his life climbing boulders, mountains, crossing streams on slippery rocks, finding frogs, lizards, and other wildlife, and making friends with other hikers. People began calling him "Little Man." Some gave him toys. One gave him a pet rock, another gave him a Hot Wheels, and another, a pocket watch.

Every morning they would wake up before six and begin their routine. During the day, Mom and Dad kept Harvey busy thinking up things to do as they hiked, like planning how to build a house, or a spaceship, or how to organize a party.

The weather got the best of them, however, in the Smoky Mountains when a serious snowstorm hit and they had to backtrack thirty miles to safety, which took two-and-a-half days!

"Harvey has boundless energy," said one hiker who accompanied them from Pennsylvania to Maine. "He's plenty strong and tough. So often we'd get to camp, and I'd be beaten and tired, and Little Man would say, 'Let's go play freeze tag!'"

One of the hikers organized a treasure hunt for Harvey, hiding toys and glow sticks, drawing maps for him along the way. Said another eighty-two-year-old veteran hiker, "It's going to change his life forever, and his parents too. The kid went through some hardships, but don't we all? Hardships make us stronger. That kid is going to smile through life."

During their 209 days (seven months) on the trail, Harvey turned five years old (2021). When they reached the end at Mt. Katahdin, Maine, Harvey had to hurry back home to Virginia so he could start kindergarten! (Jonathan Franklin, "He Hiked 2,100 Miles In 209 Days To Complete The Appalachian Trail. He's Only 5," NPR, https://1ref.us/248)

Harvey Sutton
2016–

"The wilderness and the wasteland shall be glad for them, and the desert shall rejoice and blossom as the rose.... Strengthen the weak hands, and make firm the feeble knees. Say to those who are fearful-hearted, 'Be strong, do not fear'" (Isa. 35:1, 3–4).

TEACH Services, Inc.
P U B L I S H I N G
www.TEACHServices.com • (800) 367-1844

We invite you to view the complete
selection of titles we publish at:
www.TEACHServices.com

We encourage you to write us
with your thoughts about this,
or any other book we publish at:
info@TEACHServices.com

TEACH Services' titles may be purchased in
bulk quantities for educational, fund-raising,
business, or promotional use.
bulksales@TEACHServices.com

Finally, if you are interested in seeing
your own book in print, please contact us at:
publishing@TEACHServices.com
We are happy to review your manuscript at no charge.

www.ingramcontent.com/pod-product-compliance
Lightning Source LLC
Chambersburg PA
CBHW050929240426
43671CB00019B/2962